HORSE OWNER'S

HANDBOOK

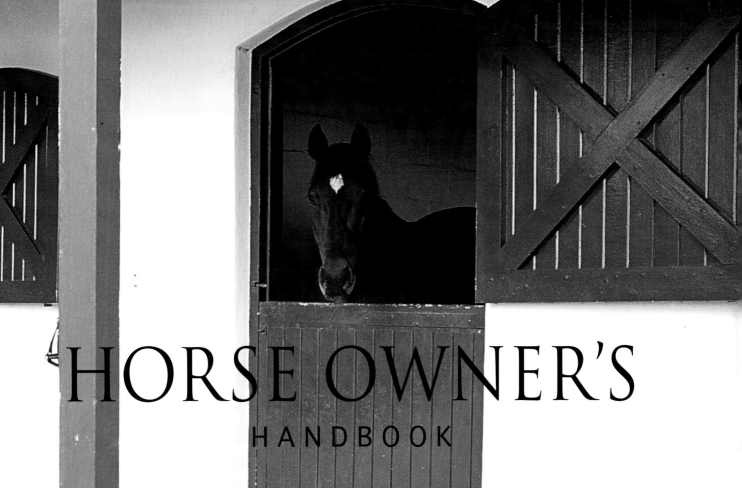

HORSE OWNER'S
HANDBOOK

PENNY SWIFT

NH
NEW
HOLLAND

First published in 2003 by New Holland (Publishers) Ltd
London · Cape Town · Sydney · Auckland
www.newhollandpublishers.com

86 Edgware Road	14 Aquatic Drive
London	Frenchs Forest
W2 2EA	NSW 2086
United Kingdom	Australia

80 McKenzie Street	218 Lake Road
Cape Town	North Cote
8001	Auckland
South Africa	New Zealand

ISBN 1 84330 446 5 (HB)
ISBN 1 84330 445 7 (PB)

Publisher: Mariëlle Renssen
Publishing Managers: Claudia Dos Santos, Simon Pooley
Studio Manager: Richard MacArthur
Commissioning Editor: Alfred LeMaitre
Editor: Roxanne Reid
Designer: Lyndall du Toit
Illustrator: Steven Felmore
Proofreader: Melany McCallum
Picture Researcher: Karla Kik
Production: Myrna Collins
Consultant: Bernadette Faurie

Reproduction by Unifoto
Printed and bound in Singapore by Tien Wah Press

d e d i c a t i o n

For Kate and the

special ponies and

horses in her life –

Caramel, Nordic Ice,

Matilda, Huckleberry

Finn, Kochra Bannut,

Napoleon, The

Leprechaun, Stag

Dinner, Beldale

Warrior and Hot Moon.

p h o t o   c r e d i t s
Corday, Sylvia: (Anthony Reynolds) p 101 top.
Houghton, Kit: p 16 top; p 61 left; p 109 top.
Langrish, Bob: Front cover (main); p 19 bottom; p 32 top; pp 44–45; p 73 top, middle, bottom;
p 81; p 87 top; p 90 left; p 115; p 116 top; p 118 bottom.

Acknowledgements

Producing a book of this nature involves a team effort, and I thank everyone whose involvement has made it possible. Without listing them all, I must single out editor Roxanne Reid, Lyndall du Toit, whose superb design elevates the book into a class of its own, and photographer Janek Szymanowski, who has captured the essence of the horse within the limitations of a very specific brief.

Numerous horse owners and trainers assisted in getting the right shot: providing horses, allowing us access to stables and riding facilities, and posing for photographs. Since horses, like children, are unpredictable, the patience of those involved is much appreciated. Tina Farr deserves a special word for getting Tanja Kyle's beautiful Warmblood, Wise Guy, to stand on command, without a halter, for pictures of a well-conformed horse. Tina and others assisted with breed pictures, including Hans de Leeuw, Pieter Hugo, Herma Jansen, Louise Pitt, Riaan Steenkamp and Lynn Greaves, whose beautiful gentle giant of a Clydesdale, Pleans Kelsy, proves the versatility of these big working horses.

A huge number of people opened their establishments and private properties to us. We thank Lynn Rowand of Nova Zonnestraal, Laura Smith of Lane Stables, Kim Wallace of the Hout Bay Riding Centre, Sharon van der Dussen of Howberry Farm, Judy Louw of Glenellen Farm, Rose Bartlett of Riverside Equestrian Centre, Lynette Mouton of Deltacrest, Derek Southey of Farm France, Cheryl Barry and Chantal Gouveia of Simonsdal Equestrian Centre, Michelle Cooke of Waterloo Bridge, as well as Lesley and Bernard Ashton, Nicolette Dunbar, Donné Evans, Anne and Barry Kleu, Nikki Mamacos, Mike and Travis Rideout, Roy Rixon, Barbara Stewart and Lisa van der Linde. Riders and horse owners who kindly posed for pictures include Evelyne Doak, Donné and her daughter Ashlea Evans (and their beloved horse Harley Davidson), farrier Philip Kotze and his wife Penny, Laurie Nicholson, Sophie Poland, Madelaine Roussouw, Georgina Rowand, Denton Sander, James Duncan, Sarah Wallace, Emily and Clare van der Linde, Kaylee Stewart and Alicia Oakes, Victoria and Lee Dunbar, Josi Nel, Andrew van der Dussen, Kira Akermann, Bianca Wrankmore and Bianca Gallant.

Thanks to Andy McPherson of Lairds Saddlery for the loan of tack for photography, and to Belinda Thom. Thanks also to David Wilken for making his luxurious horsebox available for photography, and to Michelle Scholefield for ideas and support.

I sincerely acknowledge all the people who have so willingly shared their equine knowledge over the years. Special thanks to Dr Vere Allin, who went out of his way to assist with setting up photographs of a veterinary nature and also checked the relevant text for accuracy; and to Duncan Webster of Equi-Feeds for checking the section on feed. 'Horse whisperer', Malan du Toit is a mine of information and knowledge; and we thank him for allowing us to photograph him in action.

Finally, a big thank you to our daughter Kate Szymanowski, not only for helping with photography (often out of sight), but for ensuring that horses have remained a very special part of our lives.

contents

A New Horse for You

Horse riding is a growing sport. More and more people worldwide are buying their own horses and ponies for show jumping, dressage and cross country, as well as distance riding and various games on horseback.

Riders of all ages come from widely varied walks of life and live in diverse areas in different circumstances, both urban and rural. Wherever you live, and whatever your reason for buying a horse, you will discover that the thrill and excitement of owning one for the first time is immense. Before you take the final step, however, there are many factors to be considered.

A well-fenced field with adequate grazing is ideal for horses living out during the day. You will also need to find suitable stabling and make sure you have access to areas where you can ride safely.

The decision to buy a horse is a commitment that should not be taken lightly. In addition to serious financial considerations, be aware of the time that you or your child will need to spend exercising and taking care of the animal. Even if you have the resources to pay other people to do much of the work for you, horses are a huge responsibility and they can be very time consuming. Since we generally keep domesticated horses in an unnatural habitat, away from the herd, where they cannot fend for themselves, they are totally dependent on man. In addition, horses usually live longer than dogs, cats and other domestic pets, and can be a burden in old age.

If you are planning to buy a pony or horse for your child or teenager, you may know even less about them than they do. If you are going to keep the horse at home, you need to gain some specialized knowledge beforehand and to find out which experts you can call on to help you when necessary. Alternatively, you must find a suitable and reliable livery yard or riding stables where you can keep the horse and ride.

The type of horse or pony you buy will depend on who is going to ride him and for what purpose. This narrows down the suitable breeds from which to choose, as well as the size and temperament of the horse or pony you are looking for. Your riding experience and skill will also be a determining factor, as will the price you are willing to pay.

Remember that if you are prepared to make the effort, horses and ponies can be highly rewarding animals that will bring you much joy and pleasure, even if you do not ride yourself.

HORSE BREEDS AND TYPES

Although there are never any guarantees, different breeds do have different talents and it is well worth considering the known characteristics of the world's most popular breeds before you buy. There are official breed societies in all countries, and pure-bred horses and ponies will usually be registered with these societies, as well as with the relevant stud books. Generally, registered horses and ponies are more expensive than those that are not registered. If they have good breeding, they command an even higher price. However, when it comes to competitive equestrian sports, the price tag of animals that excel is immediately raised whether they are registered or not. By the same token, a horse with excellent breeding may sell for next to nothing simply because it has not achieved what it was bred to do.

If you are buying a child's first pony, remember that many children ride unregistered, cross-bred ponies quite happily and with great success. Also, since indigenous breeds developed many of their characteristics over generations in response to climate and specific local conditions, and are therefore well adapted to a particular country, you may want a breed that evolved in your part of the world. Many countries lay claim to their own horse and pony breeds. Southern Africa's Nooitgedacht is one example of a local breed, whereas in the British Isles there are no less than nine native breeds of pony, including the little Shetland, the sure-footed Connemara – which is Ireland's only indigenous breed – and the pony that has undoubtedly had the most impact worldwide, the Welsh Pony.

THE MAIN BREEDS AND TYPES

Thoroughbreds

Although bred to race, Thoroughbreds may often move from the racetrack to the show-jumping arena and have had international success in eventing. Generally agile and alert, this is also a popular breed for drag hunting with the hounds and for hacking. Although its breeding can be traced back more than three centuries to three Arab stallions imported into England from the East at the turn of the 18th century, the name Thoroughbred first appeared in the British Stud Book in 1821. When a horse is described as 'half-bred', only one of its parents is a full Thoroughbred.

Arabians

Universally accepted as the world's oldest pure-breed horses, Arabians are bred for racing and for endurance riding in Arab nations and many other parts of the world. Originally a product of the desert, they are known for their remarkable stamina and wonderful temperament, as well as their intelligence. They are gentle and affectionate, not to mention remarkably brave. Anglo-Arabs combine the best of Arabian and Thoroughbred breeds and are commonly found in show jumping and eventing.

Warmbloods

There are many different varieties of Warmblood, all of which have generally been developed over many years as a result of introducing Thoroghbred blood to indigenous working breeds. They are bred specifically for modern equestrian sports, especially dressage and show jumping. Warmblood breeding is a huge industry, particularly in Europe, so expect to pay handsomely for a well-bred Warmblood anywhere in the world.

The breeding of Warmbloods is carefully controlled and only approved stallions may be used. However, the success of artificial insemination has led to dramatic changes worldwide, technically giving every breeder access to the very best stallions. Warmbloods are usually categorized by their country of origin – **Dutch Warmblood, Belgian Warmblood, Irish Sport Horse,** and so on. In Germany, different bloodlines have been established in different areas or at particular studs, so there is a wide variety of **German Sport Horses**. These include one of Germany's oldest Warmbloods, the **Holsteiner**, which takes its name from the district of Holstein, and the **Hanoverian**, originally bred from Holsteiner stallions and various mares, including English Thoroughbreds. The Hanoverian was named after George, Elector of Hanover, who became George I of England in 1714. The French **Selle Française** was originally bred from imported Thoroughbred sires and native mares, and later also from Arabs and Anglo-Arabs,. It differs from most Warmbloods in the use of fast-trotting stock. Its success in international show jumping is well established.

Early Warmbloods were generally heavier than Thoroughbreds, but lighter than heavy draught horses.

Appaloosa

This is an American spotted breed that has captured the imagination of horse lovers for centuries and is still used as a stock horse today. It is fast and has stamina, which makes it an ideal endurance horse. Its conformation (*see* page 17) also makes this breed of horse well suited to more graceful events like dressage or its Western equivalent, which is known as reining. Appaloosa ponies are popular with children.

Saddlebred Horses

Also known as American Saddlers in many parts of the world, Saddlebred Horses are highly popular as show horses, both under saddle and in harness. They are dubbed 'the peacocks of the show ring'. Unlike traditional British show horses, Saddlers have a high-stepping gait, which is emphasized by allowing the foot to grow long and shoeing with specially-made heavy horsehoes. Saddlebred horses are ideal for both pleasure and trail riding, and they are sometimes also seen in the show-jumping arena.

American Quarter Horses

This is the oldest all-American breed, originating in colonial America in the early 17th century when it was used as a work horse, pulling wagons and herding cattle. Compact and heavily muscled, it soon proved its abilities in sprint racing, running shorter distances more rapidly than any other breeds. This same speed and agility makes the American Quarter Horse ideal for Western-style riding, from rodeo to reining. It also makes an excellent trail rider. Part-bred Quarter Horses, crossed for instance with Thoroughbreds, make popular pleasure horses in various parts of the world.

Waler

Intended for work on the sheep stations in Australia, these horses were bred from the first horses imported into Australia – initially Cape Horses from South Africa and later Thoroughbreds, Arabs and Anglo-Arabs. Although they are not terribly fast, they are agile animals and have remarkable stamina, which makes them exceptional working horses. The Waler's successor, the modern Australian Stock Horse, has some Quarter Horse blood.

Nooitgedacht

Another good all-rounder, this breed is a worthy descendant of Lesotho's Basuto Pony and the product of a selective breeding programme in South Africa launched in the 1950s. The horses' intelligence, as well as their wonderful temperament, strong physical qualities and versatility, have recently led to demand for them in other parts of the world, particularly Australia. All Nooitgedachts are branded on their necks with the stud letters and a number.

Welsh Ponies

Welsh Ponies (and the larger **Welsh Cob**, *see* left) are now bred throughout the Western world and come in various guises and sizes, as defined in the original British Welsh Cob and Pony Society Studbook. The breed is hardy and inherently sound, and a good number have had successful showing, show jumping, dressage and eventing careers in many parts of the world. Smaller Welsh ponies make ideal first ponies, while larger Welsh ponies are often good in harness, as well as under saddle.

CONFORMATION

Horses and ponies come in all sizes, colours and shapes. Some look pretty or cute, while others appear awesome. Just as people's physical attributes vary, so do those of any horse. But unless you know what you are looking at – or for – you may not be able to rely on your own judgement alone. Some people have, or develop, a good 'eye for a horse'. By comparing horses and consciously studying their movements over a period of time, you will sooner or later be able to form a reasonably accurate assessment of their potential.

Conformation – the way a horse is formed – means more than breed and affects both looks and performance. A thorough knowledge of conformation is invaluable when buying any horse. This does not mean you need to demand perfection; you just need to ensure that the horse is well proportioned and balanced and that he can do, or has the potential to do, what you require. If there are undesirable features or visible physical defects, be sure these will not affect what you need the horse to do or his long-term health.

POINTS OF A HORSE

Above: These draught horses are a popular tourist attraction, used as a reminder of a mode of transport from a bygone era.

Below: Although Clydesdale horses are more commonly used as draught horses, this young gelding, with typically silky feathers on his long legs, is in fact used for general riding.

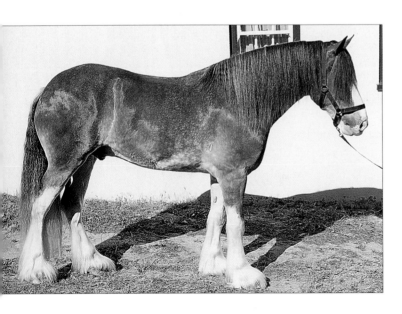

Different breeds have physical attributes that make them better suited to different functions and types of equestrian sport. For instance, the Dutch Warmblood is typically 1.63m or 16hh (hands), with a medium-length neck, strong shoulders and well-muscled quarters, enabling it to perform well in dressage competitions. Its hock joints are also well formed and low to the ground to gain propulsion when jumping. Heavy draught horses, used not so long ago in industry and still today for agriculture, are built quite differently to horses that excel in modern Olympic equestrian sports, such as dressage, show jumping and eventing, and cannot be compared with one another. The incredibly strong Shire Horse, one of the largest breeds in the world, has a long neck and deep shoulders, apparently made to carry a collar.

The world's biggest horse is the Percheron, which originated in France, though the largest came from the United States and measured 2.13m or 21hh. It has more prominent withers than most draught horses and short, powerful legs. One of the most elegant of heavy horses, it is also built for work.

If you are looking for a horse for jumping, you will not even consider a draught horse. Instead, you need a horse that has balance and a good shoulder. He should be supple over the head, neck and back, athletic enough to cope with the height and spread of fences, and agile enough to negotiate tight corners on the flat in a jump-off. A degree of boldness, coupled with a good temperament and good sense, is also essential.

Whereas a dressage horse should be bold and athletic, he must be obedient. He also needs strong hindquarters and a well-set neck that will enable you to achieve good contact.

Many breeds, including the Warmblood, have been produced to cater for a range of activities. The Thoroughbred, originally bred for racing, is now used extensively for all equestrian activities. It has a lighter, more athletic frame than many other breeds. Those with slightly shorter (short-coupled) bodies often make particularly good jumpers.

Below: The ideal dressage horse must be well co-ordinated, with good natural paces.

Above: Warmbloods, bred for equine sports, are a popular choice with show jumpers.

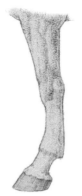

A well-conformed front leg

Over at the knee

Back at the knee

Short, upright pastern

Long, sloping pastern

FRONT LEGS AND PASTERNS

Apart from specific features that apply to different breeds, there are also certain physical features that may be applied to all horses. For instance, it is considered that small **eyes** indicate nervousness or a bad temper, although this has not been proved. A horse with large, prominent eyes is more likely to be confident and friendly.

General balance and proportion are also good indicators. Stand a short distance from the horse and ask the person holding him to make him stand square. His feet should be 'at each corner', his **shoulders** should slope, his limbs should be straight and his head and neck well proportioned. Unless the horse or pony is very young, the highest point of the

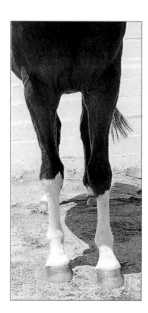

Rounded deep chest and broad flat knees

Well-formed rear

Cow hocks with points turning in

Bowed (sickle) hocks with toes turning in

BACK LEGS

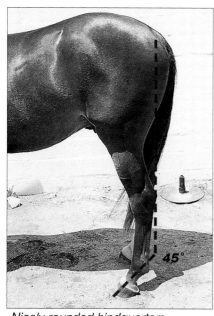
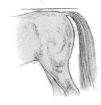
Croup too straight and tail too high

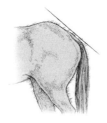

Hindquarters slope too much

Hind leg is too bent

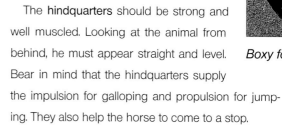
Hind leg is too straight

Nicely rounded hindquarters

SIDE-VIEW OF HINDQUARTERS

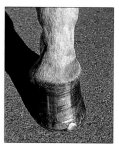
Boxy foot

withers (ridge between the shoulder blades) should be higher than the **croup** (hindquarters or rump). He should also stand with his **hocks** (joints between stifle and fetlock) well under him, so that a line dropped from the buttock to the point of the hock continues down the back of the cannon bone (between the hock and fetlock) to the ground. A horse with a broad, flat wither and heavy or 'loaded' shoulder will tend to have poor balance and you may have some difficulty fitting a saddle correctly.

Look for a fairly broad **chest**, avoiding horses with narrow chests, which could indicate poor stamina and respiratory problems. Broad, flat **knees** are also preferable to small, round 'calf knees'. The **cannon bone** on the lower part of the leg should be short and flat and free of lumps and bumps. Bear in mind that a proportionally long cannon bone could lead to tendon problems. The **fetlock joint** (ankle behind the pastern joint) should also be flat, not round or puffy. The **pastern bone** (front part of the foot between fetlock and hoof) should slope at approximately 45 degrees. If it is short and upright, and is combined with poor feet, it may lead to lameness problems. The **feet** should be in proportion to the size of the animal and should slope gently. Generally, avoid upright 'boxy' feet and 'pigeon' toes.

The **hindquarters** should be strong and well muscled. Looking at the animal from behind, he must appear straight and level. Bear in mind that the hindquarters supply the impulsion for galloping and propulsion for jumping. They also help the horse to come to a stop.

Do not confuse lack of muscle condition with a fault in conformation, and remember that many young horses grow in 'steps': the front end grows, then the back end, then the front end grows again. This means that while the horse is growing, he tends to look uneven and gangly, and you will not be able to gauge his conformation as accurately as when he is fully mature.

Finally, it is advisable to consider temperament. A nasty, nervy or timid animal is unlikely to be a good bet, irrespective of what you plan to do with him.

COLOURS AND MARKINGS

A universal system of colour classifications and markings enables horses to be described in exactly the same way all over the world. This is essential for relative standardization of identification documents – breeding papers, passports, and so on.

Colour classifications relate not only to the horse's body hair or his coat and to the points – that is, the muzzle, mane, tail, extremities of the legs and tips of the ears – but also to his eyes and hooves. Most markings relate specifically to the face and legs, although some breeds, such as Appaloosas and Paint Horses, do have body markings.

Hair colour determines the horse's official colour. The classic definitions are: black, brown, bay, grey and chestnut. For a horse to be described as black, the body (excluding any markings) and points are black. A brown horse has dark brown and sometimes almost black points. A bay horse has black mane, tail and points, and is a lighter, more reddish brown than a 'brown' horse, although this can range from very light tan to dark mahogany. A chestnut is lighter in colour than a bay, and generally more golden. Its mane and tail may be darker or lighter than the body colour, but never black. A liver chestnut is a lightish brown colour.

Horses are never described as white, although some 'greys', as they are generally referred to, do become very white, especially as they get older. Greys range from a dark iron hue, in which black hairs are predominant, to white. A 'dappled grey' horse has a grey mottled coat with darker patches. In a 'flea-bitten' grey, the white coat is spattered with dark hairs all over.

More exotic colours include roan, dun and palomino. Horses with white hair mixed throughout the coat are described as roan. This 'colour' is categorized as strawberry roan if the white is mixed with chestnut, red roan if a bay coat is mixed with white hairs, or blue or grey roan if a brown or black coat is mixed with white.

Horses come in many colours. Seen here are (from left) black, roan, chestnut, brown, grey, bay.

The coat of a dun horse ranges from a light yellowish colour to various shades of brown. The points are black and there is often a dark 'list' or black 'eel' stripe down the back. There are sometimes also zebra-like markings on the legs.

Palomino horses are golden-cream – sometimes dun-like – in colour, but with a pale cream or flaxen mane and tail. Interestingly, even though the American Palomino Horse Association defines ideal 'breed standards', palomino is a colour type and not a breed.

1. **Bay:** mane, tail and lower legs are black; body varying shades of reddish-brown
2. **Black:** completely black, except for white markings
3. **Brown:** coat of black and brown hairs; mane and tail dark brown or almost black
4. **Dun:** yellowish- to grey-brown coat with black points and stripe
5. **Roan:** any basic colour mixed with white
6. Variegated (coloured) coat: spots, patches and patterns of various colours
7. **Grey:** ranges from dark iron-grey to white; may also be dappled or flea-bitten
8. **Chestnut:** light brown to gold; mane and tail are never black

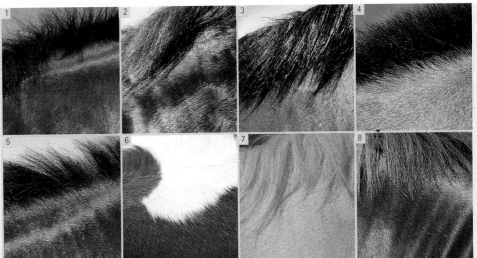

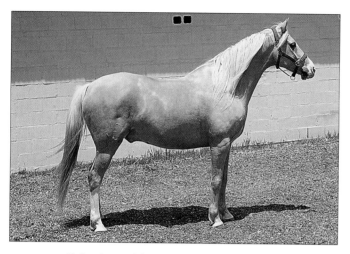

Palomino: golden-cream with a flaxen mane and tail

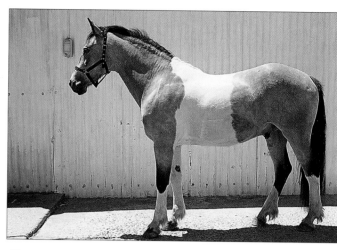

Skewbald: patches of dun, white and brown

Patches, spots and other patterns result in further colour-related descriptions. In the United Kingdom, a 'piebald' horse has large patches of black and white, while a 'skewbald' has white patches combined with any other colour except black. In the United States, these horses may be registered as either a Pinto or a Paint Horse, depending on certain specific criteria.

Some people believe colour may indicate a horse's temperament: bright chestnuts are considered fiery and spirited while dark bays are said to be sensible and reliable. However, this is an old wives' tale.

Markings are essential details when describing a horse. The most common natural markings are found on the head and legs, usually formed by white hair. Other markings include small whorls of hair, as well as flecks and spots that are only distinctive when the horse is examined up close.

Head markings include:

- *blaze*: a solid, wide white marking extending from forehead to nose
- *stripe*: covering a vertical line similar to a blaze, in other words, from the eyes to the top of the nostrils,

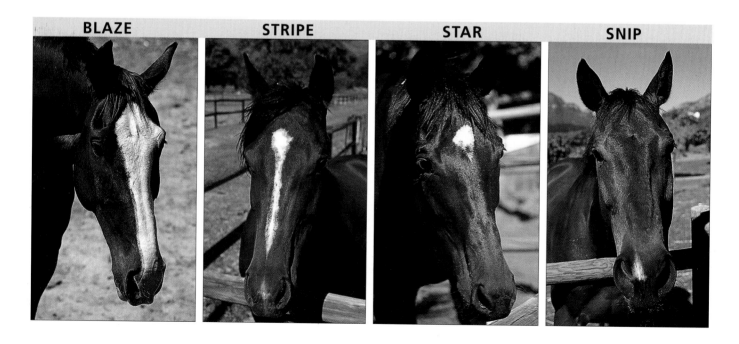

BLAZE | **STRIPE** | **STAR** | **SNIP**

but not as wide and sometimes joining a star

- *star*: a patch of white on the forehead which may be diamond- or star-shaped
- *snip*: a white patch near the lips or nostril, sometimes extending into the nostrils

Leg markings may occur on one or more legs and may differ from leg to leg. They include socks – white hair to below the knee or hock – and stockings – white hair covering the leg, the hock or even to above the knee. Ermine marks are black spots on white patches, usually above the hoof. A horse with a white sock or stocking is likely to have a pale-coloured hoof as well.

There are several spotted horse breeds, the best known being the Appaloosa, which commonly sports intricate patterns on his body, legs and sometimes his face. For descriptive and identification purposes there are five principal coat patterns: leopard (egg-shaped spots on white), snowflake (white spots, concentrated on the hips), blanket (with white or spots on the hips), marble (a mottled pattern) and frost (white specks on a dark background).

Eyes are usually brown. A wall-eye (also known as a 'glass eye') is white or blue-white in colour due to a lack of pigment, but does not affect the horse's eyesight.

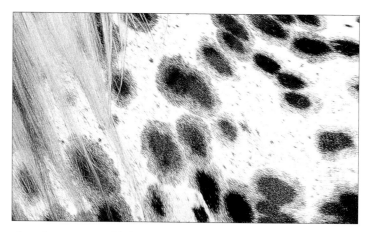

Appaloosa coat with leopard spots

Appaloosa coat with marble pattern

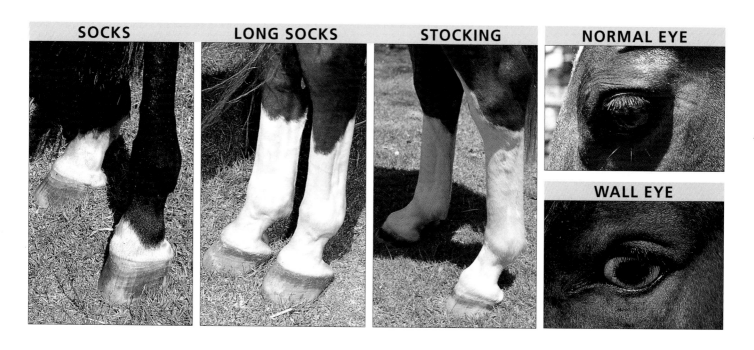

SOCKS **LONG SOCKS** **STOCKING** **NORMAL EYE**

WALL EYE

BUYING A HORSE

Most people who buy their own horses have some experience of riding, even if they are not competitive or have not had formal riding lessons. However, even if you do have some knowledge of horses, it is sensible to pay someone with greater experience to give a second or third opinion before you finally commit yourself. Riding instructors, for instance, are usually happy to give advice and will often help to find a suitable mount. If you or your child are having lessons, you should be able to trust your instructor, even if he or she is likely to receive commission from the sale.

Once you know what kind of horse or pony you want, you can decide where to start looking. There are numerous options, from dealers and breeders to riding schools and even auction sales. If you are looking for a Thoroughbred and are an experienced rider, you may consider buying one 'off the track' from a racing yard or racehorse trainer. If you want a young Warmblood or American Saddler, you would probably be best advised to contact breeders. Even if they have nothing suitable, many breeders keep track of horses they have sold and may be able to put you in touch with reputable dealers. Established and popular breeds have their own breed societies in most countries, which will be able to give you some guidance in terms of what is available for sale.

You could also try a horse charity like your local animal welfare or horse care unit. Those who rescue horses and ponies are usually willing to let them go to loving homes once they have been rehabilitated. But be careful: these horses may have been confiscated because they were being maltreated, so taking this route is not really advisable for inexperienced first-time buyers.

Right: Always try a horse or pony out before you make the final decision to buy.

Advertisements in various horse-related newspapers and magazines, or even on the Internet, are other sources of information. Be aware, however, that all kinds of people place advertisements, from dealers, agencies and breeders – reputable and otherwise – to private individuals who may be selling because they have experienced problems. Try to find out what the horse or pony has been doing and who has been riding it. You cannot rely on verbal assurances from strangers that this is, for instance, a 'bombproof' pony or horse with 'no vices'. All too often, ignorant first-time horse buyers are conned by

slick sales talk and find themselves with problems they are not equipped to cope with adequately .

You should always ride the horse at least once before making a decision. Before you get on, ask the owners to put him through his paces so that you see how he performs for someone else. If you are going to be riding on public roads, ask for the opportunity to see how the animal reacts in traffic. It is also a good idea before you take him home to see how a horse handles entering a horse box. Boxing problems are very frustrating and can take quite a long time to overcome.

If you are not totally convinced that this is the horse for you, you may be able to take him on trial for a week or two, or lease him temporarily. Never be forced into making an instant decision unless you are absolutely certain you are doing the right thing.

Below: It usually pays to ask a professional to help you choose your first horse. Ask for the opportunity to see how he reacts in different situations, with and without a rider on his back, as well as how he loads into a trailer or horse box. Never allow yourself to be forced into making an instant decision.

Financial implications

Before you decide to buy a horse or pony, it is essential to understand what is involved financially, and to assess the overall cost factor.

Buying the horse is often the cheapest part. Thereafter, you not only need to feed and stable him, but also to keep him healthy. The norm is to shoe a horse, but even if you choose not to shoe yours, you will need a farrier to visit regularly to trim his hooves. All horses also require regular deworming and inoculations, some of which may be compulsory in your part of the world. If you are stabling the horse away from home, find out whether these costs will be included in the livery, or whether added onto the monthly fee you will be charged.

A good livery yard will offer supervised stabling facilities, as well as a variety of services ranging from grooming to lungeing and exercising of horses. Vet and farrier fees will cost extra.

Tack is another cost factor to take into account, as well as blankets (rugs) and other equipment for the horse. Once purchased, these items must be maintained and replaced from time to time.

If you are going to insure your horse, which is advisable (*see* page 29), this will be yet another monthly bill to be paid.

Competitive riders, or the parents of competitive riders, will also need to cover the costs of lessons and show entries. If competitions are held away from home, there will be the added expense of getting there. While you may be able to ride to some shows, the inevitable issue of transport should be considered. This is another costly element as you will either have to pay someone to transport your horse each time or buy or hire a horse box or trailer. If it is the latter, be sure you have a vehicle that can tow it.

The vet check

Having found the horse you want, the last step is to have him checked by a veterinarian – for your own peace of mind and for insurance purposes. This may seem unnecessary, particularly if the horse appears to be sound, fit and healthy. It is, however, a safeguard that will give you a professional opinion regarding the horse's state of health and soundness, as well as an assurance that he is suitable for the work required. For instance, a good vet will pick up foot and leg problems that might have a negative impact on a prospective show jumper.

As the buyer, the onus is on you to have the horse checked and the costs of doing so will be for your account. Use a vet who regularly works with horses: the vet who normally treats your dog or cat may not necessarily be the right person to call. Never be tempted to use the seller's vet – you need a completely unbiased opinion.

If the seller has breed papers, certificates or an official passport, make these available to the vet and tell

Routine vet checks often include a flexion test on the horse's front legs. The animal is then trotted out to see if he is sound.

Horses are large creatures whose instinctive defence in the face of danger is flight. A horse that has access to public roads, for instance, is immediately at risk if he bolts, and many animals have been injured or have caused extensive damage to vehicles and property during such incidents. Even the best mannered horse becomes agitated in situations of stress so it makes sense to take precautions. Remember that if your horse causes injury to people or damage to property, you will be held legally liable, no matter where in the world you live.

You may also want to investigate the possibility of medical insurance of some sort so that veterinary bills will be at least partly covered in the event of injury or illness.

Before committing yourself to a scheme, get several quotations, preferably from a good broker who specializes in equine-related insurance, and who can offer several options.

If horse theft is a problem in your area, consider having your horse freeze-marked or branded for identification purposes. This, with any scars and natural markings like whorls, will be noted on official documentation, including your horse's passport, if he has one.

him or her for what purpose you are buying the horse. Once the vet has examined the horse you will receive a written report or certificate, whether the horse 'passes the vet' or not.

If you are buying a pony for competition purposes, you may also require a height certificate, depending on the regulations of your local horse society.

Insurance

Irrespective of the price you pay for your horse or pony, insurance should never be overlooked. Various policies are available, offering not only cover for the horse itself, but also third party and public liability, as well as cover for riders, horse boxes and tack.

Below left and right: All brands should be properly documented in your horse's passport or other papers. These are helpful for identification purposes and may identify a particular breed.

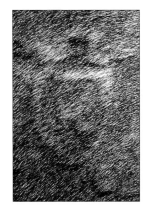
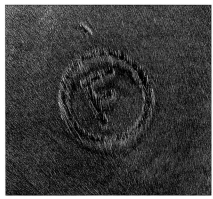

A Home for your Horse

Having made the decision to buy a horse or pony, you need to decide where to keep it. To a large extent, climate and seasonal weather conditions will determine whether you can consider the option of keeping your horse or pony at grass, without permanent access to a stable. Many ponies and horses, particularly hardy breeds, cope well as long as they have sufficient space and access to some sort of shelter, if only large trees. If there is suitable grazing and a constant supply of water, a horse in light work may thrive in this environment; after all, it is probably the closest you will get to a horse's natural habitat.

In many parts of the world it has become the norm to provide stabling of some sort, however basic, particularly for competition horses and those that are worked regularly. While some people keep their horses stabled day and night – except, of course, when they are being worked and ridden – many horse owners worldwide opt for a combined system, stabling only at night or, in hot climates, only in winter.

You can consider keeping the horse at home if you have the space and facilities or your property has the potential for creating paddocks and accommodating shelters and stables. If not, you need to find suitable facilities you can rent, or someone with a stableyard and paddocks who can provide a livery service at a fee. Either way, remember that horses are gregarious creatures with a herd instinct and they thrive on company. For this reason, it is usually best to avoid keeping one horse or pony on his own.

Above: This beautifully maintained traditional barn includes stables on the ground level.

Another consideration is where you will do most of your riding. Unless you have a horse box and the time and energy always to be transporting your horse to suitable locations, you need to have somewhere to ride either on your property or wherever the horse is to be kept. Alternatively, you need easy access to an arena and/or suitable riding country, ideally without having to cross busy roads. A circular lungeing arena, where you can exercise your horse, would also be an advantage, as would an indoor arena, particularly in cold, wet climates.

FIELDS AND PADDOCKS

The size of the field or paddock needed depends on the number of horses kept and whether they are to be stabled at night. Some horse owners, including breeders, happily leave their animals together in large, undivided fields. Provided the vegetation is suitable and fresh water is always available, they can roam free and get plenty of exercise. This is a healthy way for young horses to develop and quite a common solution for those in retirement. On the downside, horses kept together often kick and bite one another, either in play

or in establishing or enforcing the pecking order. They can also hurt themselves on fencing and branches, or on stones you may not realize are there. For this reason, horses at grass should be checked daily, especially if they are not being ridden and brought in for grooming and feeding. The International Pony Club advises its members to catch their ponies and horses and to feed tidbits once a day – this makes them easy to catch if they are not being ridden frequently. Sensible advice, since there is little as frustrating as chasing a pony around a field for half an hour or more when all you want to do is ride.

Smaller paddocks are a popular option for properties supporting larger numbers of horses that need to be separated or turned out with selected companions. This is also a common choice when employing the combined system of stabling at night and turning out by day.

Any field or paddock should be properly fenced with secure gates to keep the animals safely within the area. Some experts recommend fencing across corners so that a galloping horse will not be in danger of getting hurt at this point. In any case, dangerous areas within fields should be fenced off to prevent access and possible accident.

Horses will generally reject vegetation that does not agree with them, but it is essential to remove poisonous weeds. If necessary, get an expert to help you check the vegetation before allowing horses to graze. Be sure, too, that the vegetation is safe for grazing if weed killers have been used.

Although leaves of trees are not considered part of a normal equine diet, horses do seem to know which are safe to eat and can destroy a plant in no time at all. Bear this in mind when planting shade trees, protecting saplings until they are well established.

Left: A spacious, well-fenced field is shared by several horses turned out during the day.

Fields

Fields for horses at grass should be large and well drained, without rocky outcrops or rough, steep ledges. It is impossible to be dogmatic about the acreage required per horse, but each will need several hectares so that you can rotate areas used for grazing. Clumps of trees will provide shade although you may also wish to erect some sort of shelter from sun, wind or rain. The quality and type of grass will determine whether you need to supplement with hay or other bulk foods (*see* pages 103–107).

Water is a priority and some sort of trough must be kept constantly filled. Old baths can be suitable, provided they are secure and built into a suitable framework. Remove taps and any sharp, projecting elements. Clear leaves and other debris from the water regularly and break any ice that forms in very cold climates. A natural stream or spring, provided the water is free of additives, is one of the best supplies.

All fields should be properly maintained and managed. Horses are selective and wasteful grazers, often picking away at favourite, succulent patches that soon become bare and then muddy in rainy weather. Ideally, subdivide each area into two or more sections so that one can be rested while the others are being grazed. Farmers recommend putting sheep or cattle

Below: An automatic water feeder is an easy way to ensure that the trough is kept constantly filled.

onto the land that is not being grazed by horses. They have different preferences and will usually eat any grass the horses have spurned, along with parasites detrimental to horses. This helps to reduce worm infestation, which is an inevitable and serious problem unless all manure droppings are removed regularly. Interestingly, the horse's internal parasites have no ill effect on other livestock.

At some stage each area being grazed must be completely rested, and possibly harrowed and fertilized. This must preferably be done in early spring so that the grass has a chance to re-establish itself and grow for a month or two before horses are allowed to graze there again.

Paddocks

By definition, paddocks are small, enclosed fields, usually located near to stables. The size of each will usually be determined by the space available and the number of paddocks required. It may seem obvious that the bigger they are the better, especially if more than one horse will be turned out in each paddock. However, a bigger area can encourage spontaneous gallops and flybucking sprees, which can be quite scary for the uninitiated horse owner, especially if several horses are participating. Even more frightening is the tendency for some horses to fight over fences. To avoid this, you can incorporate narrow corridors between paddocks if you have the space. These need be no wider than 2m (6ft 6in).

Ideally, paddocks should be flat and grassed, although many a horse has spent his days in sandy or, in wet weather, muddy paddocks without ill effect. The paddocks must be without stones, and this may mean removing stones progressively as they get turned up to the surface.

Even if the paddocks are grassed, grazing will be more limited than in a large field. This will not be a problem if additional bulk foods, such as hay and straw,

are provided throughout the day for roughage. Remember that hay and/or grass normally comprise at least two-thirds of the diet of any horse or pony. Horses' stomachs are relatively small so they eat small quantities of whatever is available throughout the day.

Paddocks, like open fields, must have a permanent supply of clean water. If using smaller containers like buckets, make sure that these are topped up regularly throughout the day.

Above and below: *Corridors between smaller paddocks keep horses apart and prevent them from fighting over the fences (right).*

Arenas for exercising and schooling

Exercise arenas are a bonus for anyone keeping a horse at home. The simplest type would be a flat, grassed area. Remove all stones before using it to ride on, and topdress it regularly to encourage good grass growth.

The size of a training arena will depend on the work you do with your horse, but it should be at least 30m x 30m (98ft x 98ft) or the size of a small dressage arena – 20m x 40m (65ft x 130ft). Unfortunately, unless the ground is properly prepared before the grass is planted, the surface can be very hard, particularly for jumping. For this reason, sand arenas are sometimes preferred or, better still, sand may be mixed with rubber chips, wood shavings, bark, or a specialised polymer or gel polymer. Before the sand is brought in, the sub-base must be properly prepared, preferably by a professional.

A circular lungeing ring should be at least 20m (65ft) in diameter. If the ring is too big, it is difficult to work with the horse; if it is too small, it could lead to injury. In any case, lungeing should only be carried out by a trained person. Sand arenas are common for lungeing, although a layer of sawdust may also be spread thickly around the circular track.

Top: A standard size dressage arena.

Above: A mixture of sand and rubber chip is popular for both jumping and dressage arenas.

Below: A well-equipped practice jumping arena.

Below: A circular, sand lungeing arena with a secure post-and-rail fence is an invaluable facility for any stable yard or riding school.

Fencing

It is vital to fence fields, paddocks and arenas. Fencing should be strong, secure and high enough to discourage horses from jumping over them. If you have small ponies, ensure that they cannot wriggle through gaps or over rails.

Post-and-rail fences, with two or three rails made of poles or flat timber, are ideal for all types of equine enclosures. Alternatively, you can combine wire or heavy-duty wire mesh with upright posts or poles, but there is always a danger that horses will get their hooves caught in the wire, particularly if they start fighting across the fence. A compromise is to construct a post-and-rail fence with only the top rail of wood and several rows of high-tensile wire beneath this.

Avoid barbed wire, which is dangerous and can easily injure a horse that tries to push its way through the fence or jump it. Also avoid any other fencing with spikes, whether these are made from metal, wood or any other material.

Hedges and solid walls are suitable for enclosing paddocks, but not usually practical. Hedges take a long time to establish and walls built from stone or brick are expensive. If there are existing hedges or walls on the property, these may be incorporated in the paddock design.

Although a good rule of thumb is to ensure that the fencing is at least as high as the horse's back, bear in mind when planning paddocks that agile ponies and competition horses easily jump fence-high obstacles. Ironically, it is usually ponies that cause problems; although many horses can clear 1.4m (4ft 6in) with ease, they are seldom the ones that try to escape.

If you have problems with horses or ponies jumping fences, electrified fencing may be the answer. Available in various forms, including practical wide tape, it is securely strung between posts in addition to rails. Most horses quickly gain a healthy respect

Top: *Post-and-rail fencing is attractive and safe.*

Centre and above: *Electric fencing may be combined with rails or used on its own.*

for electrified fencing. Although battery-powered electric fencing is available, this is best kept for temporary arrangements – at shows, for instance. If you are installing a permanent electric fencing system in the paddocks, ensure that you have it connected to the mains supply by a qualified electrician.

Gates must be safe and easy for people – but obviously not for horses or ponies – to open and close. They should be hinged and hung a little way above the ground. They should always be fitted with safety catches. The only other recommended alternative is to have slip rails or movable poles set in brackets. Slip rails provide an inexpensive option but can be unwieldy in some instances.

Finally, whatever entrance you decide to have to a paddock or field, ensure that it is wide enough to enable a person to walk through it while leading a horse or pony.

A gate should be wide enough to enable vehicles to enter the paddock when necessary.

A hinged gate forms the entrance to this paddock.

Two metal gates secure a communal paddock.

Far left: A clever safety device secures a chain.

Centre: A slip rail is cheap.

Left: A chain secures the gate to a pole.

Open-plan, American barn-style stables are ideal in all weather conditions.

STABLES AND SHELTERS

In general, horses do not need elaborate housing arrangements, although there are basic requirements for stable buildings. Competition horses, including show jumpers, racehorses and polo ponies, benefit from living in a controlled environment where they are kept warm and dry and have a well-regulated diet, particularly if they are clipped in winter. You can blanket or rug them and feed extra rations to compensate for the extra energy they use to keep warm, but providing them with a snug stable is preferable.

Although field shelters are usually rustic structures that do not require electricity, lighting and power points are useful, if not essential, at any stable buildings – lighting so you can see what is going on after dark or in the early hours of morning, and plug points

(with safety covers) for tools and veterinary equipment. If you have a sick horse, you do not want to have to fumble about in the dark with a torch. Although every individual stable does not necessarily need to be lit up, you want an arrangement to illuminate the building and area immediately outside. At least one power point is indispensable. Light switches should be located outside the stable.

You should also keep a fire extinguisher readily available at the stables in case of any emergencies.

Stable structures

These come in all shapes and sizes, from simple wooden shelters to elaborate buildings incorporating tack rooms, feed storage rooms and facilities such as automatic watering devices, even air conditioning,

Left: A built-in feed trough and hay rack provide a practical feeding facility in a well-lit stable.

Above: A ceiling fan provided with a protective cover keeps the horse comfortable in hot weather.

Below: Brick stables can be built with an additional roof shelter for protection from sun and rain.

fans or heating. Of course, livery yards are just as varied in style as they are in the services they offer, so in general you can expect to get what you pay for.

If planning a stable from scratch, site it in a well-drained spot protected from prevailing winds. The idea is to provide shelter from wind, rain and excessive heat or cold, without restricting light or fresh air.

Materials that are used to build stables will depend on your needs and preferences, as well as what is permitted in your area. Check with your local authorities. Official building plans are usually required for any structures, including simple wooden structures.

There are essentially two types of stable: what is known in many countries as the 'loose box' and stalls, which are often located in an open barn. However, architectural creativity has led to a remarkably diverse range of styles, from buildings that are simply partitioned, to open barns incorporating traditional box-size stables subdivided in such a way that the horses can all see one another.

The more time a horse spends in his stable, the more important it is for him to have visible company and an interesting outlook. Bored, frustrated horses become unhappy and often develop stable vices (*see* pages 88–90.

Stalls are the smallest type of stabling – as narrow as 2m (6ft 6in). Generally, the animals are tethered in such a way that they can lie down, but not turn around or roll. In the traditional stall arrangement, each horse faces a blank wall while all the tails are towards the access passageway. This makes mucking out or cleaning the stables easier, but it is far from ideal as it is restrictive and can cause boredom.

Box-type stables are usually square in shape, and may be anything from 3m x 3.6m (10ft x 12ft) for a

These rustic stone and timber stables, with a feed room at one end, feature a small roof overhang offering protection from the elements.

small pony to 3.6m x 4.2m (12ft x 14ft) for a large horse. Stallions and foaling mares should have larger boxes, at least 4m x 5m (13ft x 16ft).

Loose box stables may be built in a row, with solid walls, and doors all facing outwards. If there is a large number of stables, they may be built in a U-shape, perhaps opening onto a courtyard. Internal walls may incorporate openings, with metal grids allowing the horses to see one another. Wooden stables may be partitioned with poles, or with partial walls that do not reach ceiling height. Ensure that any partitioning, wooden or otherwise, is strong enough to withstand a horse's kick. Horses are powerful creatures and can do a lot of damage in very little time.

If each stable has direct access outside, the stable roof should extend over the stable door, creating an overhang that will provide some shade and allow rain to run off instead of dripping inside. If a window is incorporated in the design, it should open outwards and should be protected by bars or mesh.

Only shatterproof or safety glass should be used for glazing. Stable roofs need to be relatively high – at least 3m (10ft) – so that a horse will not hurt its head, even if it rears.

Stable doors generally have two halves so the top half can be left open – hence the generic name for this type of door used in houses. However, a genuine stable door should be a little higher than most – that is, at least 2.2m (7ft), with its bottom half a little longer than the top. It should be 1.2–1.3m (at least 4ft) wide. All bolts and catches must be secure, with no projections. Check them regularly to avoid the possibility of injury to your horse. Like windows, doors should open outwards.

Remember that good ventilation is essential. Damp, dusty and stuffy stables can lead to allergies, infections and other irritations. If a stable is a little cold, a good-quality blanket or rug will provide both comfort and warmth.

Floors should be non-slip, safe and preferably non-absorbent. Concrete is commonly used as it is practical, easy to lay and relatively inexpensive. Unless the floor is waterproofed, it will absorb some moisture, so bedding will need to be cleaned and if possible moved aside daily to allow the base to dry out and air (*see* also pages 46–47).

Brick is also suitable, provided it has a smooth finish and is laid perfectly flat. Some people favour a natural earth base rather than a man-made floor. This is acceptable as long as a thick layer of bedding is

Top left: *Even horses have toys to prevent boredom.*

Top right: *This secure, well-made stable door has an anti-weaving frame attached.*

Right: *A water container is filled from the outside and then pushed through a hole into the stable.*

Above: This water trough is fitted with an automatic filling device so that the horse need never go thirsty.

Right: Straw is an economical bedding material that is favoured by many people.

provided and kept clean. You will obviously not be able to scrub the floor, but most moisture will disappear if natural drainage of the soil is good. Be warned, though, that building and/or health regulations in your area may prohibit this type of floor. Some local authorities also insist on specific drainage plans, with channels running from the stable to outside drains.

Since horses are generally fed in the stable, give some thought to the mangers and water containers that you will provide. Both should be placed low so the horse can feed and drink in his natural position, with his head down. Automatic water feeders that empty into a bucket or box are ideal, but do not fit everyone's budget. A large 20-litre (4-gall) bucket is adequate, but will need to be topped up last thing, especially on hot summer nights. If your horse tends to knock buckets and feed bins over, set the bucket in an old tyre in order to stabilize it.

A built-in manger is useful to prevent feed from being tossed into the bedding. Ideally, it should be fitted across the corner of the stable on the same wall

as the door. Hay may be provided in a hay rack or from a hay net tied to a secure ring or to grilles on windows or between the stables. If the stable is large, you can place feed hay on the floor, but keep it away from the bedding. There is always the danger that a horse or pony may get his feet caught in the hay net if it is not tied high enough. Remember to tie the hay net with a safety knot.

If your horse shows a tendency to paw at the net, rather do not use one at all. Instead, place hay on the floor or in the feed bin or manger once he has finished eating.

Right: A water container can be securely attached to the wall.
Overleaf: Straw bedding is provided for a mare and her newly-born foal.

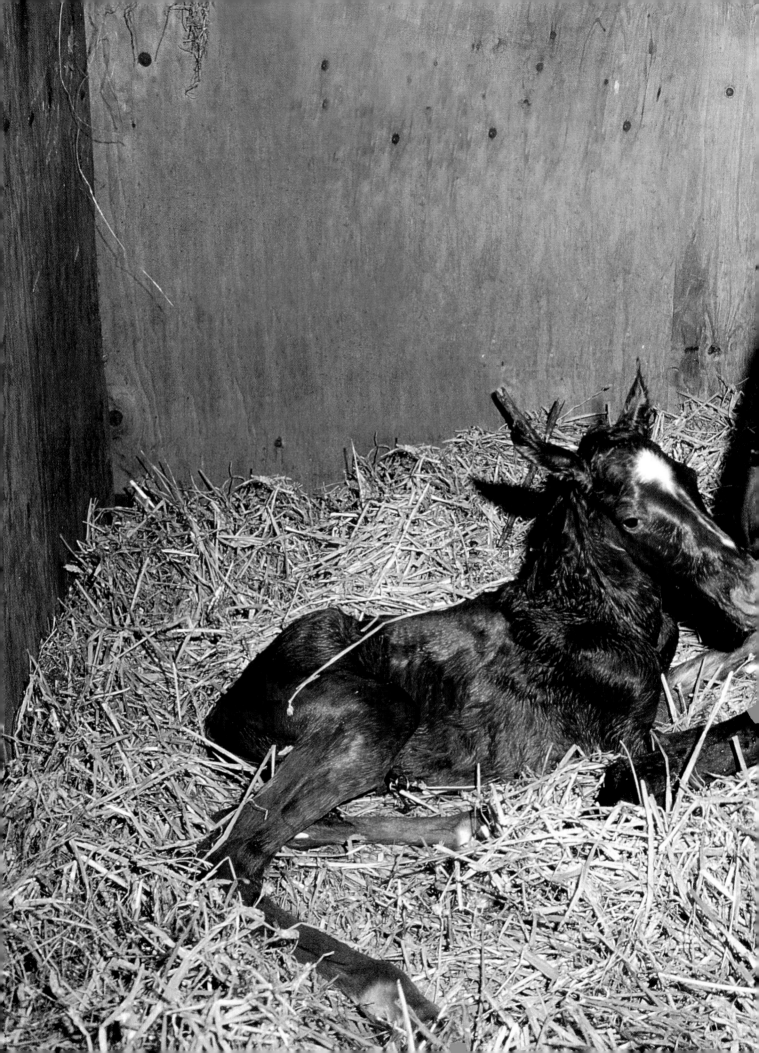

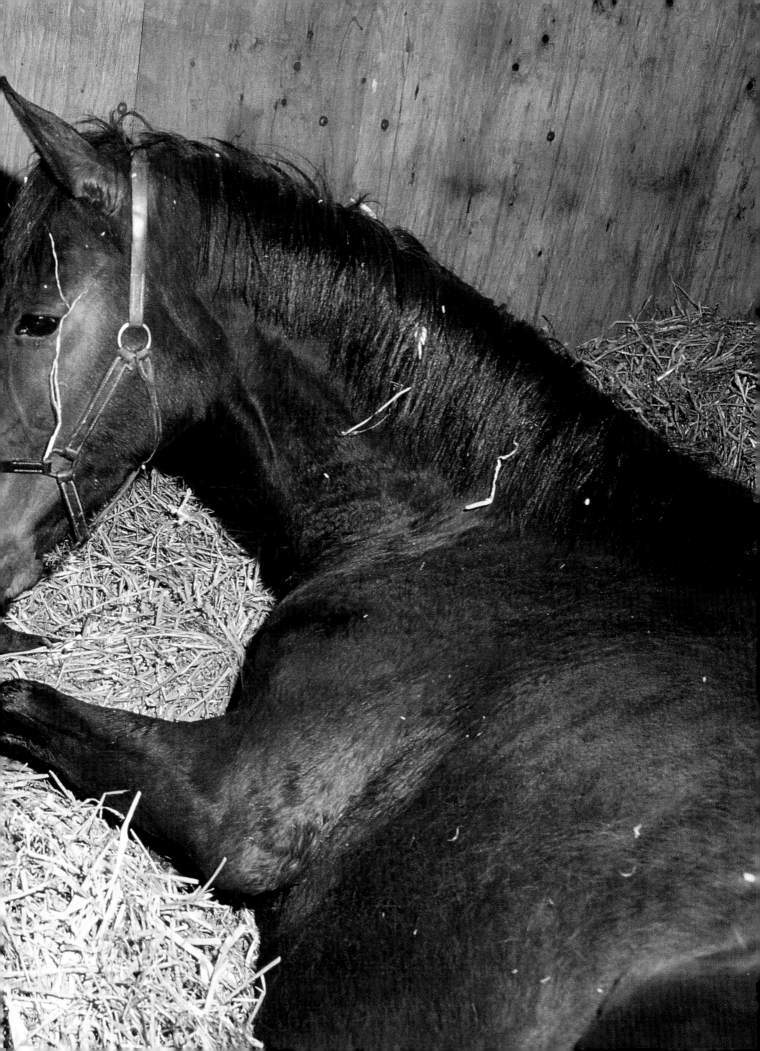

Bedding

Bedding provides a safe and comfortable place for horses and ponies to sleep. Some types also absorb moisture, including urine. Although horses often sleep on their feet, most will lie down if they feel safe and unthreatened. One of the delights for new horse owners is to peep into the stable after dark and watch their beloved animals curled up asleep or lazily blinking at them.

There are several bedding options, the two most universally popular being straw and wood shavings.

Wood shavings are a popular and practical form of bedding that is absorbent.

- *Straw* is easily obtainable and reasonably economical if you buy it in bulk, provided you have somewhere dry to store it under cover. It is warm and comfortable and easy to work with, and allows most of the urine to drain away rather than be absorbed. Disadvantages are that some people, and indeed some horses, are allergic to straw, while some greedy ponies and horses tend to eat it. Like feed, bedding straw is available in different types, depending on where you live. Wheat straw is generally the most suitable. Other types include: oat straw, which is soft and fine and tends to be the most popular straw snack; and barley straw, which is least suitable as it gets soggy more easily and often contains stiff awns or bristles that irritate the skin. On the positive side, all types of straw are easier to dispose of (*see* 'Disposing of manure and bedding' on page 48).

- *Wood shavings* provide a light, soft, manageable bed that is absorbent. Sawdust is not advisable as it can cause colic if accidentally ingested. Shavings are more difficult to dispose of naturally, as spreading them on land to be used as pasture by horses is not advisable since it can spread the eggs of worms and other internal parasites.

- *Shredded paper* is popular for bedding and good for horses with allergies, but needs to be changed more frequently than straw or shavings. It is relatively difficult to dispose of as it becomes heavy when sodden.

- *Peat* makes a comfortable bed but is an ultra-absorbent, labour-intensive material that is also comparatively dirty. It is, however, easy to dispose of – especially to gardeners.

- *Sand* is used as bedding in some countries but is not recommended: it provides no warmth, becomes compacted and can cause colic if ingested.

- *Specialized bedding materials*, including hemp, are dust-free and absorbent, but usually expensive.

MUCKING OUT AND BEDDING DOWN

1

Every morning remove all soiled bedding material and the inevitable piles of manure. Unless you are using the deep litter system (*see page 48*), turn all material methodically to uncover sodden areas as well as any manure that may be hidden underneath.

2

Move all remaining bedding to the back and sides of the stable, as far as possible separating clean straw or shavings from slightly soiled material. Use a fork and/or shovel to do this, and expose as much of the floor as you can. Scrape away any residue with the sides of the shovel.

3

Sweep the floor clean with a hard-bristled broom. From time to time you should also give the floor a good scrub with disinfectant. After sweeping and/or scrubbing, leave the bedding on the sides and allow the stable to air. Ideally, the cleaned stable should be aired all day, although this will not be possible if the horse lives in.

4

Later, spread the slightly soiled material across the floor and cover it with the clean bedding, raking to ensure the floor is evenly covered. Top with fresh straw or shavings if necessary. When laying straw, remember to shake the stalks well to separate them and ensure a nice, springy bed.

Whatever bedding is used, droppings and sodden material will need to be removed daily, the floor cleaned or 'mucked out' and fresh bedding added – preferably when the horse is outside or being ridden. There are no hard and fast rules regarding the depth of bedding used, but it should be thick enough to provide both warmth and comfort. A good rule of thumb is that if you can feel the floor through the bedding, it is not thick enough.

With what is known as the deep litter system, a permanent bed is cleaned and added to daily, but not mucked out. Start with about 150mm (6in) of shavings and add a thick straw bed on top. Remove droppings and excess moisture daily with minimal disturbance, then add fresh straw to the top of the bed. Normally, some urine will drain to the bottom, causing the base material to rot. From time to time – at least every six months – the entire bed should be removed and restarted. Note that if ventilation is adequate and you are managing the bedding properly, there should be no offensive odours. If the stable becomes smelly or musty, check the ventilation.

If your horse lives in, his stable should be mucked out thoroughly every day.

Field shelters

These provide cover for horses and ponies living out in fields or paddocks, whether they are being kept at grass or just turned out during the day. There are no doors or windows and the horses can use the shelters when and if they please. Position the field shelters to give maximum protection from prevailing winds.

The size of the structure depends on the number of animals likely to use it at any one time; it may be as big or small as you wish. Wood is the preferred construction material. Although corrugated iron sheeting may be used, it is not ideal as it is very hot. A typical shelter is open-fronted with solid sides, although shadecloth is also an option.

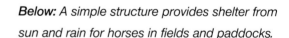

DISPOSING OF MANURE AND BEDDING

You may be able to organize for manure and soiled bedding to be removed from the stables regularly or find a way to dispose of it yourself. If you live on a farm or smallholding and have the space to keep it while it degenerates, horse manure may be kept for use in garden beds. Rather than make manure heaps, dig several holes at least 2m x 2m (6ft 6in x 6ft 6in) square and 2m (6ft 6in) deep. Throw the dung inside, together with raw fruit and vegetable waste if you wish. Once the first hole is full, leave the manure to settle and decompose while the vegetable matter rots. By the time the third or fourth hole is full you can probably start using – or perhaps even selling – the first batch. Be sure to locate manure pits away from the house and stables to avoid any odour or flies. Also make certain you are not violating any health regulations.

Bedding is a little more difficult to dispose of, although straw can be used as garden mulch or burnt when it dries out. Other types may be dug into the soil or used as fill, provided you do not immediately plan to use the ground for horses' pasture.

Below: A simple structure provides shelter from sun and rain for horses in fields and paddocks.

Tack and feed rooms

These are an invaluable addition to any stable complex. Ideally, these should be separate rooms, although in practice they are sometimes combined. Tack rooms for storing riding equipment need to be dry. They should also be securely burglar-proofed if used to store saddles and other expensive items.

Any room used for storing feed should be clean, dry and well ventilated. Ideally, hay, straw and lucerne or alfalfa should be kept in a separate barn or building away from the stables in order to minimize fire hazards near the horses. If hay and straw are to be kept in the feed room, place bales on pallets raised off the ground to prevent moisture contamination. Effective rodent control is also essential: your local authority may have specific requirements in this regard.

Top: *A metal field shelter with a shadecloth roof is ideal for hot-climate countries.*

Above right: *This immaculate tack room shows a wide range of the equipment that is available.*

Right: *A feed room should be carefully planned.*

CHAPTER THREE

Caring for your Horse

I f you have been riding at a school, or even leasing a horse or pony, you may already have some tack and riding equipment – even blankets and a basic grooming kit. If not, you will have to start from scratch.

While the tack required is determined by the type of horse you have, as well as the kind of riding you will be doing, items such as rugs, blankets, and so on are all affected more by the home you have arranged for him and the climate in which you live.

In addition to all the riding paraphernalia, you should equip yourself with a good first aid kit (*see* page 120), a selection of items required for travelling (*see* pages 94–95), and other items needed to keep your horse properly groomed and healthy.

You or a stable hand must be able to undertake daily grooming tasks, including brushing the coat and picking hooves, as well as periodically pulling manes and trimming tails and tufts of hair on the fetlocks (foot feathers). While most riders happily learn to plait their own horse's mane, relatively few clip their own horse, preferring to employ someone with the correct equipment and skills. You will also need to enlist the regular assistance of a farrier to help care for your horse's hooves and to shoe him, if required.

Horses' teeth must also be attended to periodically, either by a veterinarian and/or an equine dentist.

TACK AND EQUIPMENT

Go into any tack or saddlery shop and you will realize there is a vast array of equipment and clothing for both horse and rider: rows of different saddles and fittings; all kinds of bridles, halters and reins; bits made for different purposes from metal, rubber or synthetic materials; numnahs or saddle pads of varying shapes, sizes and colours; piles of blankets, rugs and day sheets.

Boots, bandages and leg-wraps also come in a variety of shapes and sizes, made from a range of materials. There are brushes,

A leather punch is an invaluable tool.

combs, hoof picks, rubber bands and blunt needles for plaiting; different oils for maintaining hooves or leatherware; soaps and shampoo for cleaning tack; and additional soaps and shampoos for cleaning horses. But there is no need to buy it all. Start with the essentials and then, if necessary, add to your equipment as you can afford it.

Head collars and halters

Head collars (sometimes called halters) are usually the first pieces of equipment a horse will encounter. They are made of leather or synthetic fabric, which is easier to keep clean. They usually consist of a *headpiece, noseband, cheekpieces* and *throat latch*

buckled or stitched together. The head collar is slid over the horse's nose and under the throat before being fastened over his neck, behind the ears. A simple halter is made of webbing or rope and slides over the nose and behind the ears. All types are used with a lead-rein or rope, enabling you to tie the horse up if you have to, or to lead it.

Head collar

Bridles and bits

Bridles are available in various styles and shapes and should be chosen for the job the horse is to do. Competition rules usually specify which bits and bridles may be used, so be sure to check the rule books before you compete. Generally, the simplest option that works for horse and rider is the best. For this reason, most riders should start off with a simple *snaffle bridle* comprising a leather *headpiece*. Together with *cheekpieces*, this supports the bit in the horse's mouth. The *throatlash*, made from the same piece of leather as the headpiece, helps to keep the bridle in place while a separate *browband* prevents the headpiece from slipping back.

The simplest noseband is a standard *cavesson noseband*, which fits around the nose above the bit. The *flash noseband* is a type of cavesson, but is fitted with an additional narrow strap, which is attached to the front of the noseband below the bit. It is often used in basic training, generally to help settle horses in the mouth. Note that the cavesson is the only noseband that should be used with a pelham bit or double bridle, while only cavesson or flash nosebands may be attached to *standing martingales*, which incorporate straps to keep the horse's head down.

Flash noseband

Drop noseband

Grakle noseband

Drop nosebands are fastened below the bit and are useful for stronger horses, preventing them from opening their mouths and evading the bit. The nosepiece should rest on the bony part of the nose and should not restrict the horse's breathing.

Grakle nosebands consist of two straps that cross the front of the nose over a small padded leather disc. Their action is similar to a flash noseband, and they sit well clear of the nostrils. They are most popular with event riders who find them useful for controlling their horses during the cross-country phase.

The *kineton noseband*, used with a snaffle bit, can be useful for horses that pull excessively, but should only be used by experienced riders. The action on the nose keeps the bit forward, reducing the pressure the bit would normally have on the mouth.

PARTS OF THE SNAFFLE BRIDLE

headpiece

browband

cheekpiece

cavesson noseband

reins

snaffle bit

throat latch

running martingale

TYPES OF BITS

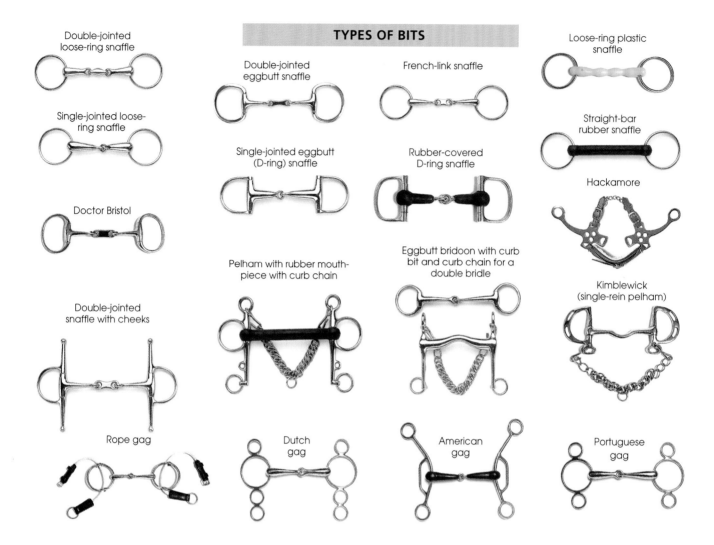

Double-jointed loose-ring snaffle

Single-jointed loose-ring snaffle

Doctor Bristol

Double-jointed snaffle with cheeks

Rope gag

Double-jointed eggbutt snaffle

Single-jointed eggbutt (D-ring) snaffle

Pelham with rubber mouth-piece with curb chain

Dutch gag

French-link snaffle

Rubber-covered D-ring snaffle

Eggbutt bridoon with curb bit and curb chain for a double bridle

American gag

Loose-ring plastic snaffle

Straight-bar rubber snaffle

Hackamore

Kimblewick (single-rein pelham)

Portuguese gag

Bits are made of stainless steel or compound metals, as well as synthetics, rubber or vulcanite. There are three main types: the *snaffle*, the *pelham* and the *curb bit* (used with a double bridle). Together with related parts of the bridle, different bits act on various parts of the mouth, as well as the nose, chin-groove and poll (top of the head). To be effective, the bit must fit properly and be used correctly. A thin bit is generally more severe than a thicker one.

A snaffle is the most commonly used bit. There are several different types, the most common being the plain, *jointed snaffle*. A single-jointed loose-ring snaffle has a mild but effective action, primarily on the lips and corners of the mouth. The *eggbutt snaffle*, which has smooth unhinged joints at the sides, has a similar

action and gives good results in horses with sensitive mouths. *D-ring snaffles*, with side rings shaped like a D rather than being round, also have a single joint in the centre, but the metal, except for the joint itself, is some-times rubber covered. A *cheek snaffle* or *fulmer* has bars on either side, which can be useful when a horse is disobedient or difficult to turn. Side pieces may be jointed or fixed. Some snaffles have a double joint, including the *French snaffle*, the *KK* (a popular German bit) and the *Doctor Bristol*, which has a rectangular central plate with squared sides that can be set at an angle to press on the tongue. As the Doctor Bristol's action is quite harsh, it not permitted for dressage, but can be useful for experienced cross-country riders on strong horses.

Twisted snaffles, including fulmers with twisted mouth elements, are very severe and not generally recommended. Various gags, including gag snaffles, use a pulley effect to raise the head and are sometimes used to control difficult or strong horses. These bits have a poll action, that is, they work on the top of the head, as well as on the lips, corners of the mouth and the tongue. They are severe, so should be employed with caution.

In addition to jointed snaffles, several *straight-bar types* are made from steel, tough vulcanite, rubber and various other synthetic materials. Be aware that some horses learn to draw their tongues away from a straight-bar snaffle bit, or push their tongues over it, negating the action of the bit.

The *pelham* is a curb bit that has a straight, curved or jointed bar with a curb-chain and may be used with single or double reins, but only with a cavesson noseband. The top rein, which is attached to the rings above the bar, acts on the mouth and tongue of the horse, while the bottom rein, fitted to larger rings below the bar, acts on the chin-groove and poll. When used with only one pair of reins, leather couplings (rein connectors) are fitted between each pair of rings. The *Kimblewic*k is a single-rein pelham, with a straight bar and small tongue-groove.

A *double bridle* incorporates two bits, a *bridoon* (which is a form of snaffle) and a curb bit, each of which acts in a different way. Commonly used by experienced dressage riders on reasonably advanced-level horses, the double bridle allows more refined use of the aids, but should only be introduced once the horse accepts the bit confidently and happily. It should not be used by novice riders or for novice horses.

Left: A double bridle has two bits.

ASSEMBLING A SNAFFLE BRIDLE

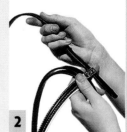

1. Thread the headpiece through one side of the browband and then the other and adjust so it is centred at the top of the headpiece.

2. Thread the long strap of the noseband through the browband and under the main headpiece, then buckle it up.

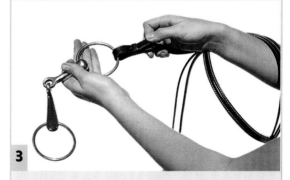

3. Buckle the two cheekpieces to the headpiece on each side before attaching these to the bit, ensuring the bit is the right way around.

4. Attach the reins to the bit rings on either side and buckle the loose ends together. Thread the flash strap through the loop on the noseband.

The *hackamore* (*see* left) is a bitless bridle that has a poll action and also acts on the nose and chin-groove. These parts of the horse are all sensitive even if there is no bit. If used incorrectly, especially by an inexperienced rider, a hackamore can be damaging and may cause serious injury.

Reins are usually made of leather and may be plain, laced or plaited. Some combine rubber with leather for a better grip. Two reins are attached, one to each side of the bit, and then buckled together.

Auxiliary equipment

Auxiliary reins and martingales are used for training and lungeing horses.

A simple *lungeing cavesson* is designed to be used with a *lunge-rein*, which is usually attached to the central ring (one of three) on the noseband. It is made with broader leather than a regular bridle and it has a well-padded noseband. When in use, the jowl-strap is buckled firmly round the horse's nose so that the cheekpieces do not pull forward during work.

Side-reins and *running reins* are also used when lungeing. When correctly adjusted, they encourage the horse to lower his head and neck and soften his back.

Martingales, used to gain extra control of the horse and stop him from raising and throwing his head, are also made of leather. Incorporating neck straps to keep them in place, martingales are looped over the girth and taken between the forelegs before being connected to the bridle or reins. A *standing martingale* is attached to the cavesson noseband (or cavesson section of a flash noseband), while a *running martingale*, which gives more freedom of movement, is connected to the reins by means of rings, allowing it to run freely up and down the reins, which should be fitted with rubber martingale-stops. An *Irish martingale* keeps the reins in place and stops them going over the horse's head.

Breastplates made of leather or webbing, sometimes with additional strapping, are attached to the front of the saddle on each side of the horse's neck and to the girth to prevent the saddle from slipping backwards. They are used by both event riders and show jumpers.

Above: *Martingales (left) and breastplates (right) are both useful auxiliary items of tack.*

FITTING A SNAFFLE BRIDLE

1 With the head collar on, slip the reins over the horse's neck.

2 Remove the head collar, maintaining slight pressure on the horse's nose.

3 Push your thumb onto the bar to open the mouth; insert the bit.

4 Carefully take the headpiece over the horse's ears.

5 Buckle the throatlash, allowing a fist space between it and the jowl.

6 the noseband, ensuring it sits just below the cheek bones.

7 Make sure the noseband sits level on both sides; adjust if necessary.

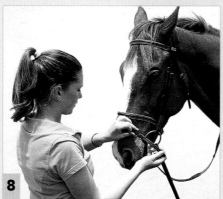

8 Pull the flash through the loop and buckle up between the bit and the loop.

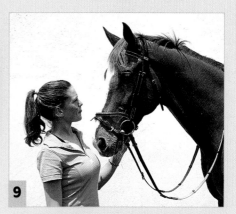

9 A good-looking, well-fitting snaffle bridle is comfortable for the horse.

Saddles

A saddle is the single most expensive item of equipment you are likely to buy and should never be purchased without being fitted to ensure it is suitable. Buy the best you can afford, ensuring it is not only comfortable for you, but also fits your horse or pony perfectly. It is better to buy a good second-hand saddle that sits properly on your horse's back than an expensive one that does not fit correctly and may even cause injury.

There are various types of saddle, but most novice riders opt for a general-purpose saddle that may be used for both flatwork (including hacking and dressage) and jumping, and for a variety of disciplines and equestrian sports, from hunting to showing. More experienced, competitive riders usually graduate to more specialized equipment made specifically to suit the discipline in which they are competing – specially designed dressage saddles, for instance.

PARTS OF THE SADDLE

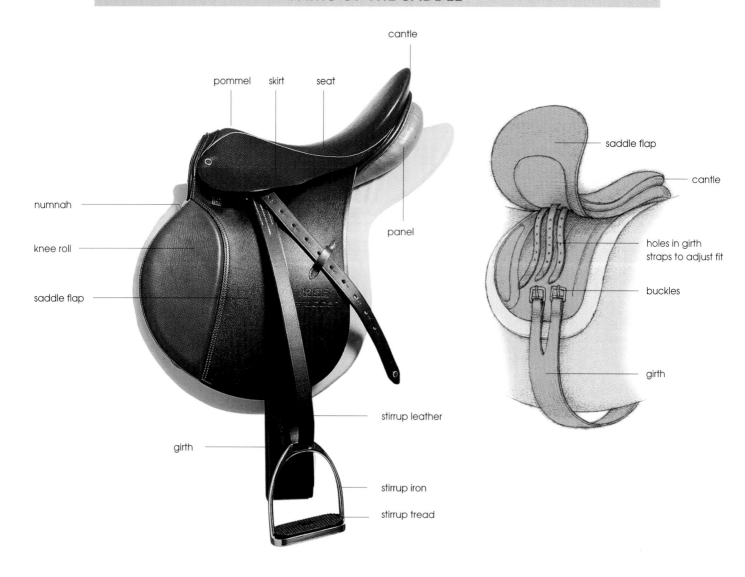

numnah

knee roll

saddle flap

girth

pommel   skirt   seat

cantle

panel

stirrup leather

stirrup iron

stirrup tread

saddle flap

cantle

holes in girth straps to adjust fit

buckles

girth

Dressage saddle   *Western-style saddle*

Although the structure of each type of saddle is slightly different, all are constructed over a frame known as a tree, the size and width of which determines the size of the saddle itself. Traditionally made from solid but pliable wood, such as beech, saddle trees are now made with laminated wood or synthetic materials. They may be rigid or sprung, in which case they are called 'sprung trees'. The seat of the saddle and the panel on the underside are shaped and padded for the comfort of both horse and rider. Most saddles are finished in leather of varying qualities, but synthetic materials are also used successfully. Buy the best quality you can afford.

Once you have chosen a saddle, you need to buy additional fittings: a suitable girth to fit snugly around your horse's belly (girth) and keep the saddle in place, stirrup leathers and stainless steel stirrup irons. *Girths*, which are sometimes padded, are made of various materials, including leather, nylon, string and webbing. Some incorporate elastic ends to improve the fit. Three girth straps are attached to the webbing, which is

- *Dressage saddles* may have a deeper seat than a general-purpose saddle. They have long, straight-cut flaps at each side to accommodate the lengthened leg position of dressage riders.

- *Jumping saddles* have relatively short, shaped flaps that are forward-cut to accommodate the rider's legs when jumping with what is known as a light seat – maintaining contact with his legs as he leans forward.

- *Close contact saddles*, which are Continental in origin, have recently become popular for jumping. As the name suggests the design of the saddle, which has less padding in the seat, allows the rider to achieve a closer contact with the horse.

- *Western saddles*, sometimes quite elaborate, are still used by working cowboys and those riding Western style, although there are considerable variations. Generally, Western saddles are heavier than English or European saddles, with a deep seat making them comfortable for riding for long periods. They are used with thick pads and blankets rather than the usual numnah or saddle pad.

- Modern *endurance saddles* combine some of the features of the traditional Western saddle with those of the lighter, general-purpose saddle.

Below: Girths are made from various materials; (from left to right) synthetic, padded, elasticated, wicking and leather (for a dressage saddle).

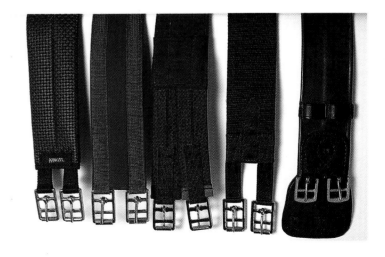

stretched over the tree on each side. For safety, the girth is buckled to two of these straps. Event riders use a *surcingle* (overgirth) in the cross country as a safeguard in case the girth breaks or the saddle slips. Similar to a girth, but usually made of webbing, it fits around the horse, over the top of the saddle and the girth. Whereas a girth may be tightened once you are mounted, the surcingle must be secured firmly beforehand.

Stirrup leathers, which may be synthetic if your saddle is made of synthetic material, and *stirrup irons*, available in different sizes to fit the foot, usually with removable rubber treads for extra grip, are usually sold separately. The leather strap is threaded through a slot at the upper end of the stirrup iron, and then buckled together at the other end to form a loop. This is slipped over the stirrup bars, which should be open-ended, and attached to the tree on each side. In the event of a fall and a rider being dragged with his foot in the stirrup iron, the stirrup leather should slip off the open-ended bar, although this is cannot be guaranteed.

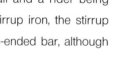

Stirrup irons

It is common practice to use a *numnah* or saddle pad – sometimes also referred to as a saddlecloth – under the saddle. This may be square, rectangular or shaped like the saddle, incorporating straps or loops that are attached to the saddle to stop it from slipping. Made from materials such as real and synthetic sheepskin, padded or quilted cotton and felt, numnahs protect the horse's back and absorb sweat while he is working. The type, colour and shape of the numnah will depend largely on the kind of riding you are doing. For instance, in competition riders generally use rectangular white saddlecloths, while riders entering showing classes sometimes choose shaped numnahs similar to the colour of the horse – usually black, white or brown. Event riders, such as racing jockeys, have their own colours and often match their clothes and skull-cap with the numnah and horse's boots.

For small children learning to ride little ponies, a felt *pad saddle*, which may or may not be covered with leather, is perfectly adequate. Relatively inexpensive, these often have no tree and just a handle for the

Above left: *A surcingle is used for eventing.*
Below: *Numnahs come in various shapes, colours and sizes.*

Below: *A simple pad saddle is ideal for a pony.*

child to hold onto, although some incorporate a tree forepart or metal arch to help the felt sit correctly on the pony's back. Pad saddles usually incorporate a webbing girth and some are fitted with D-shaped stirrups instead of removable stirrup leathers with stirrup bars. They are sometimes used in conjunction with a *crupper* – a leather strap that fits under the pony's tail and is attached to the back of the cantle to stop the pad or saddle from slipping forwards.

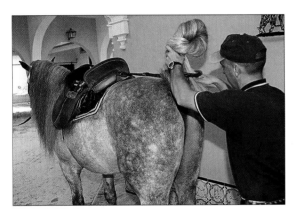

A leather crupper is fitted around the tail.

All saddles are measured across the top, from the pommel at the front (or, if it has a cut-back head, from the metal pin at the side of the pommel) to the cantle at the back. Most come in standard sizes from 38cm to 45.5cm (15in to 18in) – usually given in inches, even in countries using the metric system. They are termed narrow, medium or wide. A saddle should be fitted without a numnah or saddle pad prior to purchase: if it presses on the withers it is too wide; if it pinches the withers and spine it is too narrow. The saddle should sit flat on the horse's back, but there should be a clear passage from the back of the saddle, below the cantle through to the withers of the horse. It should always be fitted by a professional saddler.

Old saddles and those that do not fit properly can be restuffed by a saddler, but never use a saddle with a broken tree.

CHECKING THE SADDLE TREE

When buying a second-hand saddle, get an expert to check the tree. If this is twisted, cracked or broken, the saddle is useless, so do not take any chances.

- A twisted tree will injure the horse's back. Look across the top line of the saddle, from cantle (back) to pommel (front end that sits over the horse's wither), checking that it is symmetrical.

- Whether it has a rigid or 'sprung tree', you can be fairly sure that the tree is broken if the leather is wrinkled across the seat. A saddle with a rigid tree should not flex or bend at all.

- To check for a break in the front arch of the tree, it is necessary to apply strong hand pressure to each side. Although the ends will be flexible, the tree is probably broken if there is movement under the arch or around the stirrup bars, or if there are squeaking or clicking noises from these areas. If there is only a break below the stirrup bar, it may be able to be repaired.

- The cantle should also be totally rigid. If it can be twisted, the tree is broken.

- A 'sprung-tree' saddle should flex across the centre of the seat. If there is more give on one side, it could be broken. This can be checked by putting one hand under the cantle and the other under the pommel. Lift your knee above the saddle and press down on the waist (the centre of the saddle seat), trying to bend it by pulling the pommel in towards you. A well-used 'sprung tree' may have become soft, but it should still be springy.

Bandages and boots

These protect horses' legs during work, travel and even in the stable.

Over-reach or *bell boots* – so-called because they are usually bell-shaped – are made of rubber and fit around the pastern to protect the feet, particularly the heels and sensitive area just above the hoof at the base of the pastern, the coronary band. Some have straps or Velcro tape to secure them; others are simply pulled over the hooves. A horse that over-reaches can kick its own feet and injure himself if he is not wearing bell boots.

Rubber bell boots

Brushing or *splint boots* are used to protect all four lower limbs. They are made from materials such as leather or padded synthetic materials. Most have a foam lining and fasten on the outside of the leg. *Open-fronted boots* are similar to brushing boots, but designed specifically to protect vulnerable tendons. They are often used for show jumping. Thicker boots are used when eventing to give tendons extra support. *Polo boots*, which are more substantial than other boots and extend almost to the knee, are designed to protect the legs of polo ponies from sticks, polo balls and kicks from other horses during the game of polo.

Rubber bell boots are used on the front legs to prevent injury if the horse over-reaches.

LEG PROTECTION

1
Leather brushing boots with straps and buckles.

2
Colourful brushing boots secured with Velcro.

3
Tendon boots have a protective pad down the back.

4
Trucking boots help to protect legs against knocks during travel.

5
Knee caps are used to protect the knees during travel.

6
A rubber ring is used if a horse brushes on the coronet.

Travelling or *trucking boots* are designed to prevent injury while in transit. Usually made of fairly thick towelling or synthetic fibre and fastened with straps or Velcro, they either encase the leg from below the hock or just below the knee to the coronet, which they should overlap. *Knee cap guards* and *hock boots* are also made for travelling; and *tail bandages*, *tail guards* and *poll guards* should be used to protect the tails and heads of travelling horses. Tail guards are made of the same materials as trucking boots, while poll guards are generally made of leather or felt.

Stable bandages and leg-wraps are supplied in sets of four and are used to protect legs, improve circulation and keep them warm in winter. Padding (gamgee tissue, for instance) or cotton wool should be used

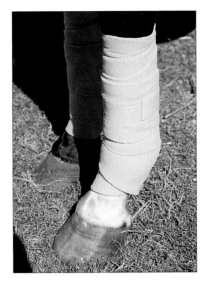

Stable bandages may be used in the event of injury or for extra warmth when travelling.

under these bandages to help equalize pressure. Put them on carefully and correctly without restricting blood flow. They should be wrapped around the leg, starting just below the knee or hock, and working downwards to the coronet; then wrapped upwards again, so that you end where you started. Secure the bandage with tape or Velcro straps, ensuring that they are not tighter than the bandage itself. The bandage should be fastened on the outside of the leg with the tail of the bandage pointing to the quarters, not the front of the horse.

Blankets and rugs

These are used in both hot and cold climates, in spite of the fact that the horse's own coat is designed to protect him. Waterproof blankets are commonly used

Cotton day sheets are used in countries with hot climates in order to protect horses from the sun.

in rainy weather and even if horses have not been clipped, they are often blanketed or rugged, if only with a sweat rug after work or competition.

Rugs, blankets and duvets are made from a multitude of materials, such as wool, cotton and synthetics. Most are secured at the chest, and with a surcingle, or fastened between the hind legs, under the tail or under the belly. Horses can be measured for their own custom-made rugs, but this is not always practical and cost-effective, so most people buy off the shelf. When buying blankets off the shelf, ensure they are snug around the chest and big enough to keep the entire body warm. Outdoor blankets should offer enough coverage to keep all parts of the body dry and protected from the wind.

Your horse's living conditions and lifestyle largely determine what is required. Breed is also a factor, although there are no hard and fast rules. Consider all the options; but if you cannot afford expensive blankets, keep your horse unclipped and rest assured that his own coat will keep him comfortable.

- *Day rugs* are made from woollen material or cotton knit and generally used between classes at com-

petitions. If they only fasten in front, they should be secured with a surcingle. Day sheets, also known as summer or fly sheets, are made from cotton sheeting and used primarily to protect horses standing in the sun all day, particularly competition show horses that could develop bleaching or pigmentations. They may also be used while travelling in hot weather, to keep horses clean and protected from the wind without providing warmth.

- *Sweat rugs and sheets* (coolers) are made of absorbent fabric, towelling or mesh and may be used alone after exercise to prevent chills, or under thicker blankets. Like day rugs, they are useful for travelling.

- *Stable rugs and duvets*, some of which are quilted, provide warmth for the horse in the stable at night. Materials that are used may include woollen or synthetic blanketing. Thickness and weight also vary. Irrespective of weight and style, the best rugs and blankets should have wicking to draw moisture away from the body. They should also be easy to wash, preferably in a washing machine.

- *Waterproof covers* used when turning horses out in

A sweat blanket made from mesh is ideal after exercise or for travelling. It also makes a good show blanket.

A fly (or day) sheet and matching fly fringe give protect from the sun − and from flies.

rainy, cool or inclement weather are often made of canvas or nylon and may be lined for warmth. Good designs incorporate neck and tail covers for extra protection. A good fit is essential if it is to remain in place when horses exercise and play in their paddocks. A popular contemporary design, originating in New Zealand and lined with warm material, has been copied worldwide and is dubbed 'the New Zealand rug'. It incorporates hind-leg straps, and its main claim to fame is that it allows clipped horses to live out all year round regardless of wind and rain.

Whatever type of rug or blanket you decide to use, learn to put it on correctly. The technique described below right is taught to Pony Club members all over the world. It makes the rug easier for a small person to handle and is ideal when dealing with young or nervous ponies and horses. Once you have formed a relationship with your horse and are sure he will not spook if you throw the blanket onto his back, you can dispense with this procedure, but it is advisable to use these tactics whenever you deal with an animal you do not know.

New Zealand-type rug, lined and fitted with straps to keep it in place. A neck rug gives extra protection from the elements.

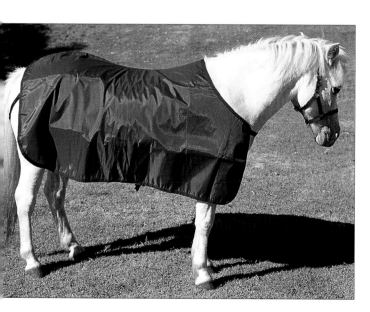

A light, unlined but waterproof rain sheet will help to keep the pony dry.

PUTTING ON A RUG

1. Tie the pony or horse up before hanging the rug over a fence, gate or stable door.
2. Fold the rug in half, bringing the back of the cover over the front.
3. Lift the rug onto the horse, holding the front of it on either side of the central seam.
4. Unfold the back section and slide it over the back of the horse.
5. First secure the front breast strap fairly loosely, then fasten the girth straps (cross surcingles).
6. Cross the leg straps under the tail and through the hind legs, and clip in place.

GROOMING EQUIPMENT

Every horse owner should have a good grooming kit. Items are relatively inexpensive and include a variety of brushes, combs and hoof picks, which should all be kept together in an easily transportable box.

- *Body brushes* with relatively fine, soft bristles are used to remove dust and flaky skin (scurf) from the coat, mane and tail.
- *Dandy brushes* have stiff, longish bristles and are used to remove caked mud and dry sweat from the coat. They are hard and should not be used on horses and ponies that have been clipped.
- *Water brushes*, which are smaller and softer than dandy brushes, are used to clean the feet, as well as the mane and tail.
- *Paintbrushes* are useful for applying hoof oil and dressing to the horse's hooves.
- *Currycombs* are made of metal, rubber and plastic. The metal ones are for cleaning body brushes and should never be used on the horse. Plastic and rubber combs are useful for loosening mud and

sweat and brushing out excess hair in winter, but should not be used on the head, tail or mane.
- *Metal and plastic mane combs* are used primarily for mane pulling and when plaiting manes and tails.
- *Sweat scrapers*, made of aluminium or plastic with a rubber edge, are used to scrape off excess water after the horse has been washed.
- *Bot knives* with curved blades and small serrations are useful for removing tiny bot eggs from the horse's legs and body. Laid by gadflies, these parasites can cause sores and worms.
- *Hoof picks* (sometimes combined with a small brush) are indispensable for cleaning out the feet.
- *Sponges* are used to clean the eyes, muzzle and solid, flesh dock of the tail. Keep these separate to avoid possible infection, particularly in the eyes.
- *Stable-rubbers, gloves or sheepskins*, although not essential, are used to give a final polish to the coat.
- *Electric clippers* are required if you plan to clip your horse yourself.

GROOMING EQUIPMENT

currycombs

sheepskins/ grooming gloves

rubber bands

water brush

bot knife

sweat scraper

tail bandage

body brush

dandy brush

scissors

hoof picks

metal and plastic mane combs

sponge

paintbrushes

water scraper

A beautifully groomed horse with glossy coat and plaited mane is ready for a show.

GROOMING AND TURN-OUT

Grooming is an essential part of stable management and vital to any horse's health and well-being. Even horses living out full time need regular attention. For instance, dried mud and sweat can clog the pores, and also cause saddle and girth sores. Regular brushing will produce a glossy coat and promote muscle tone.

Certain basic tasks should be tackled daily, while additional steps, such as shampooing and plaiting, need only be undertaken for competitions and for special occasions. In addition, tails, ears and heel feathers will need to be trimmed from time to time when they look untidy or before a show. You may opt to clip the coat once or twice a year.

Daily grooming involves removing grime and dirt and picking hooves. Brushing the coat not only keeps the animal looking clean, it also helps to keep the

skin healthy by stimulating circulation, as well as keeping troublesome external parasites, such as ticks and bot eggs, in check.

Grooming programmes vary, even for horses that are stabled. Much has to do with climatic conditions, as well as the number of horses being cared for. Some people groom first thing in the morning, while most prefer to give a thorough grooming before feeding in the evening so that the horse is clean overnight. Similarly, there are some people who advocate starting the procedure by picking out the feet; whereas others prefer to do this last. The important thing is to follow a routine that becomes familiar and comforting for the horse, bearing in mind that he is a sensitive creature who thrives on a regular routine.

The horse may be groomed in the stable or, if weather conditions allow, in the yard, in which case he will need to be tied up. Either way, it is important to remain calm and to avoid sudden movements. Talk to the horse quietly and touch him gently to indicate where you plan to work.

Generally, grooming begins by removing the worst of the dirt – mud and/or sweat – from the body and upper legs, by first loosening it with a rubber currycomb, using vigorous, circular movements. Next, start at the head with the body brush, using long, firm movements in the direction of the lie of the coat. Brush the head gently but thoroughly, taking particular care around the eyes, under the mane and forelock, under the jaw and inside the ears. Hold the metal currycomb in your free hand, using it to clean

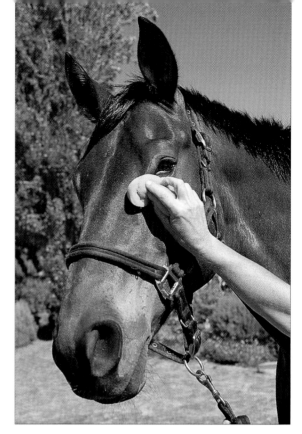

Use a clean sponge to clean the horse's eyes.

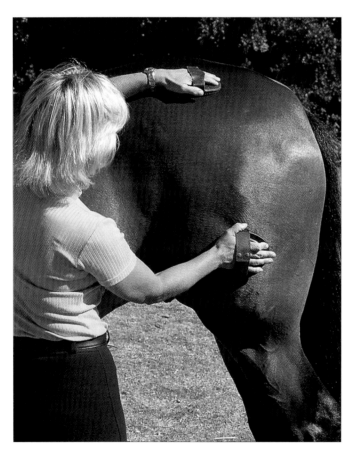

Currycombs are used to loosen sweat and other dirt from the horse's coat, but are not used on the tail or mane.

the brush every so often. To dislodge the dirt and prevent the bristles of the currycomb becoming clogged, tap it on the floor now and then, away from bedding and preferably outside the stable where the mess can be swept away later. Take care when brushing the belly and between the legs as many horses are ticklish and may react unpredictably.

Both mane and tail require special attention as excessive brushing or combing can easily break the hair. Work tangles and knots out of the mane with your fingers and then use a body brush, stroking firmly from the roots down, bearing in mind that dirt accumulates at the crest of the neck. Brush out the forelock the same way. A body brush may also be used on the tail, provided the hair is untangled first. Then hold the tail in one hand, at the base of the dock, and brush from the roots downwards. Various conditioning sprays will make the tail shiny and help prevent tangling.

You will also need to clean the eyes, mouth and nostrils with a damp sponge. A second sponge should be used to clean the fleshy dock and the skin under the tail. Even if you are sure the horse will not kick, stand to one side while you do this. To ensure the sponges are kept separate, use different colours for each end, and rinse both out frequently.

At least once a month, the sheath of stallions and geldings should also be washed to remove any discharge. Wear thin rubber gloves and use warm water and a mild soap.

At some stage during the grooming process, the underside of the hooves must be cleaned. Use a hoof pick to remove from the feet all mud and debris, including bedding and droppings. It does not take more than a few minutes and gives you the opportunity to check the feet for thrush and to ensure the shoes are secure if the horse is shod. Use the pick from heel to toe, carefully removing dirt with its point; then brush out any fine dirt or sand.

From time to time, oil the hooves – although opinions do differ on this procedure (*see* page 78). Numerous brands of hoof oil and proprietary dressings are available, and may be applied with any small paintbrush. If the feet are dirty, clean first and allow to dry thoroughly before oiling.

As a routine, horses living out only need a light brushing down. Excessive brushing of the coat removes natural greases that provide protection from the wet and cold. However, their feet need to be checked regularly and their hooves picked. Their eyes, nose, muzzle, dock and, in the case of stallions and geldings, the sheath also need to be kept clean. A grass-kept horse that competes regularly needs more thorough, more frequent grooming. Use a good quality outdoor rug to compensate for the protection that the lost natural oils and greases would give.

Quartering or 'brushing off'

This refers to a basic tidy-up, often done first thing in the morning before exercise. It does not take long and simply entails a quick brush-down to remove stable stains and excess dirt and grease. Feet are picked out at the same time.

Since nobody likes to ride a dirty horse, before exercise, the horse living out will also be given a quick going over with a dandy brush or rubber curry-comb to remove mud.

Hosing

Hosing horses and ponies in warm weather, particularly after exercise, is a ritual many grow to love. The simplest way to do this is to put the animal in a hosing dock so you have both hands free. These range from well-equipped indoor bays that are tiled and plumbed, to more simple pole structures that can be erected near to an outside tap.

Shampooing is only necessary when the horse is very dirty or before a show. Start behind the ears and avoid the face. Rinse with a hosepipe or, if you must wash in cold weather, with a bucket of warm water. Use the sweat scraper to remove excess water and rub dry with old towels.

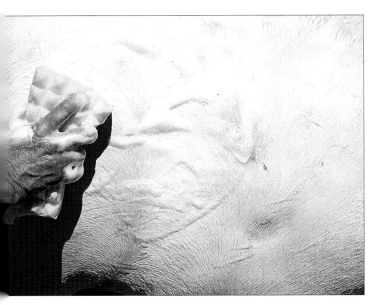

Above: Shampooing should not be done daily.
Right: A shaped sweat scraper.

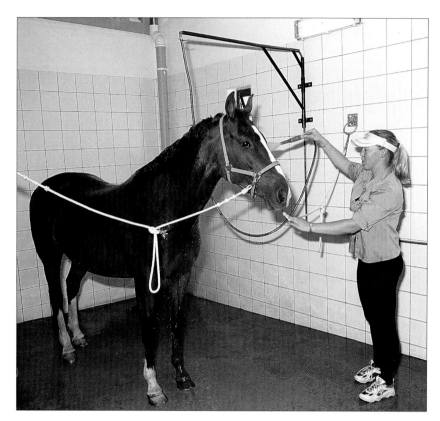

Above: A horse is hosed down in a well-equipped washbay.

Below: Horses love to roll in the dirt – even after a bath.

After exercise, muddy feet and legs, as well as the belly, should always be hosed clean. If the weather is very cold and wet, you can wipe most of the dirt off, wrap the legs in woollen bandages overnight and brush the dry mud off the next day. Do clean the feet with a little warm water and a water brush or cloth, but ensure that they are dry before the horse is stabled for the night.

Horses relish a roll after a workout, and most will head for the sandiest or muddiest patch after they have been washed. This is not a problem, as long as the mud is removed when the horse is groomed later in the day. When washing a horse before a show, prevent him from rolling by keeping the clean animal in his stable until it is time to leave.

Trimming

Trimming tails, heel feathers, long hair under the jaw and hair that sticks out of the ears smartens any horse, and does not require specialized equipment other than sharp scissors. Trimming at the poll and withers should be kept to a minimum, although it is often a practical solution when the hair is too short to plait.

Although some people trim the whiskers around the muzzle, these are sensitive 'feeler' hairs and should rather be left alone.

Tails can be 'banged' (have their ends cut off square) but do not do this with the tail in the resting position. Instead, get somebody to hold the tail in the position the horse would normally carry it when moving and bang it slightly below the hocks. If you are showing the horse, remember that a long back may be accentuated by a slightly shorter tail.

Tail hairs may also be pulled to neaten the dock end of tails that are not going to be plaited for special occasions. Using a mane comb, begin by pulling hair under the dock and then at either side. Only remove a few hairs at a time. Wind them around the comb then give a brisk, sharp pull. This may hurt, so stand on one side to avoid being kicked by a surprised horse.

Manes are pulled to thin them out and shorten them. This also helps the mane lie flat and makes it easier to plait. Start by pushing the mane comb up the shorter top layer of hair to expose the longer hairs underneath. Then wind a few longer hairs around the mane comb and pull firmly, as for the tail. Never pull the top hairs, even if they stand upright after plaiting.

If your horse hates the pulling process, it may be kinder to trim mane and tail with clippers and scissors.

Plaiting

Manes can be plaited to make the horse look neat and show off the neck and its surface line or crest, particularly for show classes and dressage competitions. The way the hair is plaited will depend on the build of the horse and the reason for plaiting. For instance, a horse entering show hunter classes will look best with chunkier plaits than a hack. Plaits for dressage may be graduated in size to show off the outline of the neck.

A horse that is lacking in neck muscle will benefit from high plaits that sit on top of the neck, while a horse with a strong crest will look best with tight plaits that sit along the neck. There are no set rules regarding the number of plaits, but traditionally there should be an odd number down the neck, plus the forelock. Remember that the more plaits you do, the longer the neck will appear. False plaits at the withers can also make the neck look longer.

Although, traditionally, mane plaits were stitched with thread to secure them, nowadays many riders use small elastic bands, manufactured specifically for plaiting, in the general colours of a horse's coat, including black, brown and white. Either way, the

The tail should be held up when it is trimmed.

hair is divided into three equal sections, which are plaited and then rolled (*see* page 74). Although not difficult, it does take practice, and there is a definite art to rolling plaits. The secret is to ensure that the hair is divided evenly so that the plaits are more or less the same size, and to plait very tightly. Dampening or gelling the hair helps. Once you have rolled the plait into a tight ball, secure with a second rubber band. With practice some people can plait and roll, using only one band for each one.

Plaiting tails takes even more expertise, patience and practice. Fortunately, riders can get away with plaiting manes and not the tail, particularly in novice classes, but this is an enviable finishing touch for the show horse.

Plait with very small bunches of hair, adding eight to ten hairs from either side of the tail as you progress, in a similar way to French plaiting. If the hair at the top of the tail is very short, or if there is not much of it, you can knot the central hairs together with thread and then use the thread to neaten the plait as you work. When you get about two-thirds of the way down the dock, stop taking hair from the sides and complete the plait with what you have in hand. Tie the end with a rubber band and then form a loop with the loose end and secure this to the rest of the plait.

If sewing, use thick, strong thread the same colour as the horse, and a blunt-ended needle with a big eye. Needles can be dangerous so work carefully.

HOW TO PLAIT A TAIL

Take three small bunches of hair from either side and from the middle, and start plaiting as for a French plait. Take a few more strands of hair from the sides as you work. Continue until almost at the base of the dock and then plait normally.

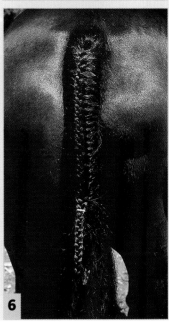

Tie up the end of the plait with a rubber band before turning the loose end under to form a neat loop. Use a second rubber band to secure the plait just below the dock of the tail.

Clipping

Clipping horses is common before and during winter as they naturally develop a thick coat that will make them sweat during work and take longer to dry off in cold or wet weather. Furthermore, a clipped coat is easier and quicker to groom and will allow the horse to work better for longer. Since the hair moults in summer, the horse should not be clipped then; even clipping in spring will spoil the summer coat.

Although electric clippers make it possible for any horse owner to clip his own horse or pony, it is not easy to clip properly. Good quality clippers are also quite expensive, so it may be better to employ someone with experience to clip for you.

There are various recognized clips, depending on the amount of work the horse is doing and on local climate. Whichever you choose, be sure to replace the coat you have removed with equine clothing, particularly if the horse lives out or is turned out during the day.

- A *full clip* means the entire coat is removed, and can take some time to complete. This type of clip is only suitable for stabled horses in full work or for those living in very mild climates.

- The *hunter clip* is common, not only for horses that hunt, but for those that are regularly worked hard. Hair is left on the legs and on a saddle patch in the middle of the back, as well as on the front of the face. Sometimes hunters are given a full clip at the beginning of winter and then the legs and saddle patch are left on at the second clipping.

- The *blanket clip* results in a patch of hair over the back – as though a furry blanket has been thrown over the horse. Every part of the horse is clipped, except this patch, the front of the face and the legs. It gives some protection, but does not look smart. In cold weather you will need to use a neck cover.

- The *trace clip* is common for stabled horses in light work and those that are driven (carriage horses) as the coat is removed from the lower neck, breast

Full clip, with saddle pad left on

Blanket clip

Low trace clip

and belly up to the point of the shoulder and across to the stifle – essentially along the line of the harness 'traces'. The coat is also removed from the tail area and buttocks, leaving the back and legs well covered so the horse looks as if he is wearing a rug and long stockings.

- The *belly clip* is useful for ponies and hardy horses living out. The hair is clipped under the belly, between the front legs and up the chest and throat.

The pattern of any clip may be marked out on the horse with chalk to help you cut correctly. If a saddle patch is to be left on the back for a hunter clip, place a shaped numnah on the back and draw around it. Clipping should start at the neck and proceed towards the rump. Use long movements against the lie of the coat, and leave the head and ears until last.

The mane and tail should never be clipped, except when the mane is hogged, which means that all mane hair is removed with clippers. This is done for appearance and, in the case of polo ponies, to keep the mane out of the way. If it is to be kept hogged, this procedure should be repeated every three or four weeks. Remember that a hogged mane will take about two years to regrow fully.

This horse, which is regularly used to play polo, has a neatly hogged mane.

PLAITING AND PULLING A MANE

1 Hold the ends of the longest hairs under the mane and push the shorter top hairs up with the comb.

2 Wind a few hairs around the mane comb, then pluck them out with one quick movement.

3 Divide the mane into a series of pigtails and tie each one loosely with a small rubber band.

4 Remove each band before plaiting the hair. Make sure it is tight at the crest roots and plait tightly.

5 For high plaits, start plaiting 3cm (1in) from the roots. To keep the plaits neat, moisten or use a little gel.

6 Secure the end of each plait with a band. Wind around several times until tight to prevent it loosening.

7 Tuck the end of each plait underneath before rolling it. Loop a rubber band around the ball to secure.

8 A series of small, neatly rolled plaits along the crest of a bay horse's neck defines the shape of the neck.

FEET AND HOOVES

Remember the age-old maxim 'no foot, no horse'. Feet problems will lead to lameness, and a lame horse cannot be ridden. It is therefore essential for every horse owner to understand the structure of the foot and be aware of what can go wrong.

Regular visits from a farrier are essential; even if your horse is not shod, the hooves will need to be trimmed. However, you cannot rely on your farrier alone; you will have to attend to your horse's feet, picking out the hooves at least once a day to ensure that the feet remain healthy. Check for stones, as well as any injury, such as puncture wounds or bruising. In addition, check for cracking and thrush (*see* page 127). Take immediate action if anything is wrong.

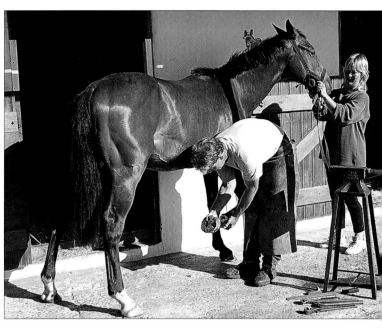

A farrier checks a horse's hooves before he begins the task of shoeing the feet.

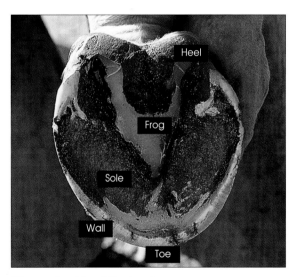

The underside of the hoof

A horse's foot consists of three parts – the wall, sole and frog. The wall is horny and non-sensitive, while the frog and sole comprise both horny and sensitive parts. The interior of the foot contains sensitive, fleshy tissue as well as blood and nerves.

When the horse's foot is on the ground we see the wall, which extends from the coronet at the top of the hoof, just as a fingernail grows from the cuticle. The

toe (the thickest part of the wall, at the front of the hoof), quarters (on each side) and heel (at the back) are all part of the wall. The slightly concave sole under the foot provides some protection, but is thin and can be bruised or injured by sharp stones and hard ground. The rubbery frog, which is rather like a natural shock absorber and anti-slip pad, has a groove or cleft down the middle, giving the horse a better foothold.

When the horse moves, irrespective of speed or gait, the heel should always meet the ground first, so that it and the frog absorb most of the weight.

Hooves, like fingernails, are constantly growing; it takes about six months for a new hoof wall to grow. Whether or not the horse is shod, hooves need to be trimmed and rasped regularly, which also helps prevent chipping and cracking.

A cracked hoof

Shoeing

The ancient Romans were the first to shoe their horses, and the basic principles have changed very little. Today, professional farriers serve an apprenticeship of three to four years and must pass an examination. Be sure that you use a qualified farrier as bad shoeing can result in injury and disfigurement.

Shoeing protects the foot, particularly when the horse is ridden on roads and hard ground, and provides a means of improving the grip on the ground with the addition of studs. Horseshoes may also be used for medical reasons, in the case of injury or to remedy an abnormality.

Shoes should be replaced every four to six weeks, depending on the work the horse does and the hardness of the ground he works on. You will soon learn how to assess when shoes are worn out or loose, or when the foot has grown too long. Check the clenches and clips regularly to ensure the shoe has not twisted. Use the tip of a hoof pick between shoe and hoof to check the shoe fits snugly. If it is not loose or worn, but the horn has grown over the edges, your farrier may refit the same shoes after trimming the hooves. If a horse throws a shoe, try to find it – particularly if he was shod recently.

There are various types of horseshoes, from thin aluminium shoes used on racehorses to heavy shoes for working heavy horses. Your farrier will advise on the best design and weight for your horse.

The traditional method of hot shoeing is still practised by skilled farriers today and involves making the shoe from raw iron and shaping it to the horse's foot while it is hot. Traditionally, this method is preferred, but is not always practical, even though portable forges are available.

Modern shoes are machine made and simply adjusted by the farrier to fit the horse. Referred to as cold shoeing, this enables the farrier to work at the stable rather than having the horse brought to him. The shoe is nailed to the insensitive wall of the hoof

COLD SHOEING

The farrier examines the horse's foot before he starts work. This young horse has never been shod before.

Before the foot can be shod, it must be clean, so the farrier picks out all the mud and dirt from the foot using a hoof pick.

Now he cleans out the frog and trims any ragged parts of the sole. Then he will use a rasp to create a level bearing surface.

Choosing a shoe that is the correct weight, size and shape for the work the horse is to do, he nails it to the foot.

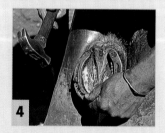

The protruding nail ends are turned over and twisted off to form clenches. The rasp is then used to neaten the edges.

1

Above: When using the hot shoeing method, the shoe is made to fit the foot. While the farrier trims and rasps the horse's hooves, the shoes are heated in a small, portable forge.

3

2

Above: The farrier places the red-hot shoe on the bottom of the horse's foot. The mark left by the hot metal indicates where the foot and shoe make contact, showing where he needs to alter the shape of the shoe or rasp the foot further.

Top right: The farrier shapes the hot horseshoes on his portable anvil to ensure that they fit each of the horse's hooves.

4

Above: Although the shoe is red-hot when it is placed on the foot, the heat does not cause pain.

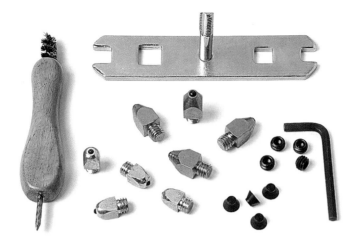

Items from a stud kit include two different types of studs, sleepers and tools used to insert and remove the studs and clean the stud holes.

with specially designed horseshoe nails. The ends that protrude through the wall are turned over and bent downwards to form a clench, which is neatened with a rasp. Many farriers recommend using horseshoes with quarter- and/or toe-clips to keep the shoe in place more securely.

If you are competing in cross-country competitions or riding on slippery ground, it is advisable to use studs. Your farrier will need to make holes in the shoes to accommodate the studs. He will usually ask in advance if these are required, and whether you want them in all the shoes or only the hind ones, which is the norm. He will help you decide what is best for you and your horse. Stud kits contain a variety of studs — big, small, pointed or chunky — as well as the tools required to insert and remove them. They are also available loose. Never leave studs in the shoes after working or competing, and unless the shoes are soon going to be replaced, always plug the holes with

Tar is applied to the foot sole.

greased cottonwool or with sleepers to prevent dirt and sand getting in the thread.

Once the horse has been shod, the farrier will ask you to trot the horse out to ensure that he is level and not sore or lame. Run alongside the horse with a long, loose lead rein. If he is not balanced, the farrier will rectify the problem immediately.

The shoes of horses that are not being worked for more than a month may be removed so the hooves can grow naturally without interference. Usually, the farrier will remove shoes for you, unless there is an emergency and the shoe has, for instance, twisted out of place or has become dangerously loose and could harm the foot. Ask him to show you how to remove the shoe correctly. It must be eased off gently after the clenches have been straightened, or cut off. Shoes must never be ripped off even if they are loose.

Oiling and dressing

This is a surprisingly controversial subject. Some people recommend oiling brittle hooves with a proprietary brand of hoof oil daily, while others insist that this simply creates a greasy film that attracts dirt. Although some people prefer the old-fashioned mixture of hoof oil and Stockholm tar, by far the most common and sensible approach is to use proprietary hoof dressings, applied according to the manufacturer's instructions.

Hoof oils and dressings are painted onto the wall of the hoof. Stockholm tar, used successfully to treat thrush and other diseases and to keep the hoof dry, should be applied to the sole of the foot, particularly in the cleft of the frog.

A good rule is to keep the hoof dry when conditions are wet and prevent it from drying out when the weather is hot.

It is essential to trot a horse out after it has been shod to ensure that it is level and sound.

EXERCISE AND FITNESS

All horses need regular exercise to remain fit and healthy. Horses in the wild have plenty of room to gallop and get rid of accumulated energy. Stabled horses and those kept in restricted paddocks will need to be ridden and exercised regularly. If your horse is kept in a field, and there is sufficient space, he will have the opportunity to run around at will and may get plenty of exercise, but this does not mean he will necessarily be fit for work.

Top left: A horse is worked out in the arena.
Above: Hacking is fun for horse and rider, keeping them both fit and healthy.
Below: Regular exercise is essential.

Event horses must be ultrafit for competition.

Hacking and schooling both contribute towards general fitness, but the programme you follow will depend on the time you have available, as well as the work you intend to do with your horse. For instance, if you are planning to event competitively, your horse needs to be considerably fitter than one required only for outrides at weekends. The dressage horse needs to be strong and muscular, so concentrate on achieving this. When you are getting a horse fit for jumping competitions, do not be tempted to jump excessively at home. Rather concentrate on steady flatwork, walking, trotting and cantering, and practising all the things you have learned in your riding lessons.

Remember that the more frequently you ride, the fitter you and your horse will become. However, unless you are preparing for endurance riding, this does not mean that you have to ride for long periods or even that you have to ride every day. Most

GETTING YOUR HORSE FIT

If the horse is simply out of condition, it will take you six to eight weeks to get him back to reasonable fitness. A horse that has been off for three or four months will take at least the same period to get fit again. Remember your horse is an athlete and muscular strength will need to be built up slowly. Never rush a fitness programme: give the horse one day off a week.

1. Start by walking for 15 to 30 minutes, increasing gradually until you are walking for about an hour. This can take about three weeks -- or even months if the horse has been resting because of a sprain or tendon injury. Horses become sound long before damaged tissue has been sufficiently repaired to withstand the stresses of normal work.

2. Introduce short periods of trot-work to begin building muscle tone. Combine this with periods of brisk walking, particularly up hills. Steady trotting on a hard road surface can be beneficial, but do not overdo this. Continue this way for about six weeks, increasing the trot-work to as long as two hours. In the case of a tendon or ligament injury, the trotting-walking phase should not start too soon and should continue for at least two to three months, but not for more than 30 minutes at a time. Eventually, introduce some slow cantering on the flat.

3. Now you can begin with serious schooling, and introduce some jumping if you wish. Increase the hill work and take him for a steady canter once or twice a week. Always start at a walk for about 15 minutes, then trot for a while before cantering. End with walking on a nice, loose rein.

instructors will assist in designing a fitness plan for your horse, which will include regular exercising, as well as riding and schooling.

If your horse has been off owing to illness or injury, it is vital that you to take great care to bring him back into work only very gradually.

CHAPTER FOUR

Handling your Horse

Horses are physically strong and must therefore be handled correctly. If you are an inexperienced rider, always buy a horse that has been broken in, is familiar with humans and used to being ridden. Be aware, though, that he may have had earlier bad experiences you do not know about, which could result in problematic behaviour. Although horses are rarely aggressive, they can be easily frightened. Sudden movements and loud noises can spook the best-behaved animal and cause it to panic. Faced with a memory of danger, it may also react unpredictably.

Remember that the inherent instinct of any horse is flight: rather than stay and fight, he will flee as far from danger as quickly as possible. As a result, you should learn all you can about horses' behaviour and take every safety precaution when dealing with them. They are gregarious animals and thrive on being with their own kind. They are also creatures of habit. If your horse has a set routine and at least one stablemate, along with food, warmth and lots of love, he will be easier to handle.

THE RIGHT APPROACH

Always approach and move around horses confidently, slowly and quietly. Speak firmly and kindly and never shout or behave in an aggressive manner, however frustrated or angry you may be. Kindness and patience will help develop your horse's good qualities; insensitive handling achieves the opposite.

When entering the stable, use your voice to let him know you are there and hold your hand out to give him the opportunity to smell you. Brush your hand firmly over his lower neck or shoulder, without patting, and avoid looking him directly in the eye. Most horses will move their nostrils over your hand as they familiarize themselves with your scent. They are inquisitive animals and are unlikely to turn their back on you unless they are fearful or angry for some reason. If they do, get out of the way as a swift kick may follow.

When approaching the horse in the paddock, move from the front towards his shoulder at the side and speak before touching him, just as you would in the stable. Generally, you should not stand directly in front of or directly behind horses, especially if you are not familiar with their behaviour.

It is customary to approach, as well as lead, mount and dismount, from the near side of the horse – that is, the left side of the horse.

When grooming, always touch the horse first to reassure him and maintain the contact until you start brushing. When picking up his feet, run your hand down his body and legs before attempting to lift them. When lifting the foreleg, stay close and face the hindquarters. If the horse will not lift his foot, lean against his shoulder and push his weight onto the other leg. It usually helps to use your voice: say 'up' or 'foot' and squeeze the joint. It may also help to press your elbow behind the knee. Make sure the hoof is under your fingers at the toe.

When lifting the hindleg, face the rear and stay close to his hip. Lean against the thigh as you pull the foot upwards, cupping your hand around the wall of the foot. Be careful not to lift the foot too high as this is likely to unbalance him and he may kick out.

LEADING

It is customary to lead a horse from the 'near' or left-hand side, especially one you do not know. Nonetheless, your horse must get used to being led from either side as there may be times that it is safer to be on the right. For instance, since you should always lead or ride a horse in the same direction in which the traffic is travelling, if you live in a country where cars drive on the left-hand side of the road, you will need to lead him on the right so that you are between the horse and the cars. If you do lead a horse on the road, use a bridle instead of a halter to make the horse more submissive and give you more control.

When leading a horse wearing a halter, clip a rope or lead rein to the halter and hold it firmly, about 50cm (20in) from the halter, with the free end in your other

SENSORY SYSTEMS OF A HORSE

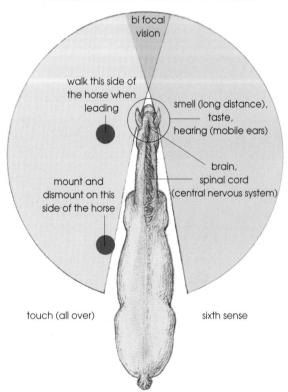

bi focal vision

walk this side of the horse when leading

smell (long distance), taste, hearing (mobile ears)

mount and dismount on this side of the horse

brain, spinal cord (central nervous system)

touch (all over)   sixth sense

Above: An obedient horse can be led easily.

Below: Take extra care when riding on the road.

hand. Never wind the lead rein around your hand – if the horse shies or rears, it could rip your fingers.

A trained horse will walk alongside you, often without even being asked to 'walk on'. If he does not oblige, do not tug and pull; rather ask someone to walk on the other side, behind him, or use a dressage whip in your other hand to tap his flank behind your back. He may get a fright, so be ready for his reaction. When turning, stay on the outside of the turn. At all times ensure that he is at your shoulder.

Above all, take note of what is going on around you. Cars, other horses and loud noises can all cause a horse to spook. Also, many things which we do not notice or pay attention to can be scary to even the most intrepid horse, so be aware of plastic bags, barrels, brightly coloured road cones and any rubbish that may be lying around.

Leading a horse in showing classes takes a little more skill, although the procedure is essentially the same. If the horse is in a bridle, stand on the near side and bring the reins over his head. Use your right hand

to hold the reins fairly close to the horse's head, with one finger between them. Hold the buckle end in the other hand. Never loop your arm through the reins as you could be dragged if the horse spooks or bolts.

If you need to lead a horse when mounted, keep the horse to be led on your left and take the reins in your left hand, holding them about halfway down with one finger between the two reins. Keep your hand as close to your knee as possible. If the horse gets agitated or frisky, shorten the rein.

Whether you are on foot or mounted when leading a horse that is tacked up with saddle and bridle, make sure that the stirrup-irons have been 'run up' and are secure so they do not bounce around. Ideally, you should also use a surcingle strapped over the saddle to keep the saddle flaps secure and ensure the saddle does not slip. For safety's sake, remove running martingales from the reins and secure to the neckstrap.

RESTRAINT

There are times that a horse or pony may need to be tied up, for example, when he is washed, clipped or examined by a vet. Ensure that whatever you tie him to is safe and secure. Always use a quick-release knot that can be undone with one tug, so that if he panics and tries to break free you can release the knot instantly. Since this is always a possibility, it is important for all stable yards to be securely and safely fenced or walled. Some lead ropes are specially designed to release in the event of a sudden or violent movement, which helps to minimize the risk of injury to horse or handler.

Sometimes people tie horses up at horse shows. You will soon discover if

Pull to release

Clip on halter

A quick-release knot

your horse has the temperament to stand in a relaxed, untroubled manner. Even if he does, though, ensure that someone is with him all the time. Share the task with another rider or horse owner, taking turns to watch each other's horse. Dreadful accidents can occur when horses escape and run off in panic. This is usually because they get a fright, at which point their instinctive reaction is almost always flight.

Never be tempted to tie a horse to his hay net; if he breaks free and runs, he could step in the net and hurt himself. Also, never leave a horse tied up alone for any length of time.

Tethering horses and ponies with a long rope while grazing is not recommended. If you have to tether for some reason − for instance, to restrain a little pony that constantly escapes under paddock fencing − ensure there is shelter and plenty of water within easy reach and always use rope with a low breaking point. This should only be a temporary measure. Never leave a pony tethered for any length of time; check on him frequently as it is all too easy for a tethered animal to wrap himself around trees and other obstructions.

EQUINE BEHAVIOUR

You can learn a lot about horses from facial expressions and body language, as well as from the sounds they make. Like human beings, they respond to smell, touch and noise, as well as to what they see. If you familiarize yourself with common equine responses and relate these to your own horse or pony, you will soon get to know him and recognize his signals.

Body language

We can learn about horses from their body language. Ears are probably the biggest giveaway, telling you when your horse is content, bored, unhappy or angry. A happy, attentive horse will have both ears pricked upwards and towards whatever he is concentrating on. While you are riding, one ear will often turn back

This horse is displaying aggression by flattening his ears against his head.

so that he can hear your voice aids. However, a relaxed horse may have floppy ears. If they do not perk up when he is shown attention, he may be sick. Whenever a horse flattens his ears against his head, he is usually angry or frightened.

The tail may also indicate a horse's state of mind. A tail flattened against the buttocks shows fear, anger or animosity, whereas a slightly arched tail that swings softly to keep away flies shows the horse is relaxed and content. A fast-swishing tail may indicate dislike or anger. An excited horse may gallop with his tail out, and Arabians and horses with Arab blood often arch their tails backwards over their quarters (rump) when they are excited.

A horse's eyes indicate mood and feelings in a wonderfully expressive way. Calm eyes show contentment while wide-open eyes usually indicate excitement or fear. As eyes are at the sides of their heads, horses have a much wider peripheral vision than man. However, a horse cannot see directly behind and will turn

Right: Flehmen is a comical expression.

away or back off if you get too close – one reason to approach a horse from the side.

Horses have a well-developed sense of smell, which they use to select food and recognize other horses. Flared nostrils usually mean excitement, possibly anger. Wrinkled nostrils indicate discomfort or irritation. Sometimes horses curl their lips and lift their heads in what appears to be a comical expression known as 'flehmen' (a German word). They are, in fact, using the Jacobsen's organ at the back of their noses to examine an interesting, unusual or unpleasant smell. By curling the top lip, the horse can close off the nostrils and trap the air he has sniffed. Stallions may do this when they scent a mare in season.

Head carriage is another indication of mood or condition. For instance, if the head is hung low or unnaturally raised, it could mean the horse is sick or uncomfortable. When standing, weight should be on all four legs, although horses often do rest a hind leg. If he rests a foreleg it may be an indication of injury.

Sounds made by horses range from a variety of neighs to snorts and squeals, some indicating pleasure, others discontent. While we cannot attach actual meaning to any sound, it is often obvious that one horse is greeting or calling to another. Many give a soft purr-like snort when you visit them in the stable or take them food, apparently indicating their appreciation. Some horses seem to grunt while exercising, either through exertion or as an expression of willingness to please.

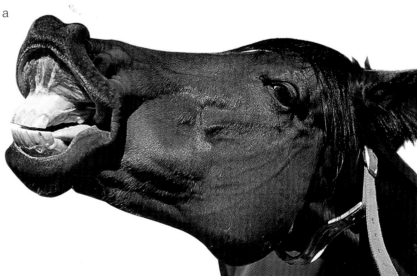

Horses love to roll. For them, this is nature's way of grooming. You will soon notice when they intend to roll, as they become restless and look down and paw at the chosen spot. They may also seem uneasy. Once a horse has rolled, he will have a good shake. If he does not, or if he does not get up, he may have colic (*see* page 119). Never allow a saddled horse to roll; he could damage the saddle tree.

Vices

Behaviour such as crib biting, wind sucking and weaving can frequently be caused by boredom or distress, or from being permanently cooped up in a stable. It may also be copied from another horse. If you notice your horse developing any of these habits, take steps to rectify the problem before the vice becomes established. If you let him repeat the habit, it becomes more and more reinforced; if, however, you can prevent it from happening, most horses will eventually forget.

If you buy a horse that already has some form of stable vice, he may have been incorrectly handled or badly trained. Any horse kept on his own will become bored and easily develop bad habits. Although there are no absolutes, be aware of potential difficulties.

- *Crib biting*, when horses gnaw at any wood in the stable or paddock, can lead to wind sucking. Usually attributed to boredom, it may also be caused by anxiety or simply by the taste and inviting smell of unseasoned wood. You need to do whatever you can to stop the horse from chewing the wood. Sometimes, temporarily covering the wood that has already been chewed, perhaps with a blanket, and placing a hay net nearby will do the trick. Otherwise, you could paint the wood with a branded, ton-toxic application recommended by your vet. Covering wooden edges with metal will also prevent crib biting, but this is an expensive option and one that is impractical in the paddock. Horses kept well exercised and content and in the company of other horses are less likely to develop this habit.

Even a special collar does not stop this horse from trying to wind suck.

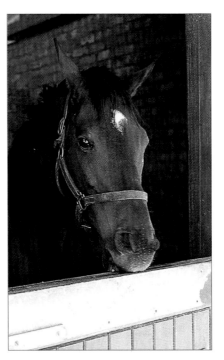

A metal plate on the door stops the horse from chewing the wood.

A special device on the stable door helps to prevent weaving.

• *Weaving* most commonly affects more highly strung horses: they stand at the door of their box or stable and sway from side to side, often moving their weight from one front leg to the other. Like crib biting and wind sucking, it is usually caused by boredom and a lack of sufficient exercise. Once the habit is formed, it is hard to break, even with plenty of work every day. In extreme cases, it can even lead to unsoundness as their feet and legs become sore. It is a habit that may be mimicked by other horses in the yard, so take immediate action. Anti-weaving frames may be fixed to the top of stable doors, allowing the horse to look out but not move from side to side. Alternatively, allow the horse to live out for a while if this is possible — he will seldom weave in a natural environment.

• *Kicking, pawing and stamping* generally reflect bad management. Confident, bold handling will often overcome the problem.

Sometimes, horses kick the door at feed time because they are hungry and impatient, or because they want to be let out into the paddock. Try to avoid the issue by feeding promptly and letting him out first. One recommended remedy is to close the top of the stable door as soon as the horse starts banging. This may teach him that kicking the door does not result in pleasure. Less easy to control is the horse that turns his quarters towards you whenever you enter the stable — threatening you with a kick. Since this can be extremely dangerous, you may need to bring in the experts. With confidence, an experienced handler will probably easily rectify this habit.

• *Wind sucking* is more difficult to cure than to prevent, so avoid buying a horse that bites the wood with his

Left: *Wind-sucking collar.*
Below: *A horse kicks out in the paddock.*

incisor teeth and then sucks in air. It affects digestion and makes it difficult to keep the horse in good condition. Special collars made of leather or metal – or a combination of the two – prevent the horse from arching his neck and, because they press on the windpipe, stop him from swallowing air. They do not prevent the horse from eating and drinking normally so they can be worn all the time, except when the horse is being worked.

- *Biting* is more common with stallions and young colts than the horses first-time horse owners are likely to buy. Some handlers believe the horse is biting from fear, so instead of severe discipline, they stroke the muzzle to distract the horse, talking gently at the same time and even blowing softly into the nostrils. Whatever approach is taken, it is important to act immediately – the horse needs to associate any punishment directly with the 'crime'.

- *Eating bedding and droppings* is usually related to diet and more often than not occurs with straw bedding. Make sure there is sufficient bulk, fibre

and salt in the diet and keep the stable clean. If you must use straw, sprinkle a disinfectant on the bedding to discourage the horse from nibbling. It may also help to mix any new bedding into the existing bedding. Ensure there is always a hay net available with fresh hay, straw, lucerne and/or alfalfa, and offer a salt lick.

- *Rearing* up on the hind legs is not related to stable management and is particularly difficult to deal with. An old wives' tale recommends breaking an egg on the head of a horse that is about to rear. However, when faced with this kind of behaviour, few riders will be able to take this kind of action. The best advice is to call in those who have experience in dealing with the problem. Let somebody you trust assess the situation and help you overcome it sensibly. Often good horsemanship, especially light hands and strong legs, will go a long way towards breaking the habit.

Left: *A horse that rears will be difficult to handle, and you may need to call in an expert to help you.*

Below: *A cheeky pony nips a horse over the fence.*

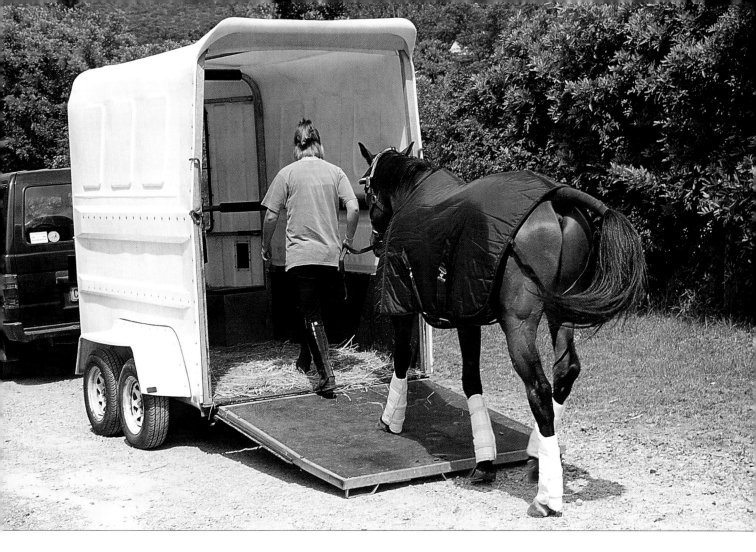

TRANSPORTATION

Transporting horses requires care and experience. It is an exacting task that needs to be tackled properly and responsibly. You may decide to hire a reputable horse transport service, which will provide an experienced driver, but if you decide to transport your horse yourself, be aware of the pitfalls of travelling too fast, and practise with an empty horsebox to get the feel of towing. Although accidents do happen, the best advice is to be prepared and forever careful.

You may never have to transport a horse yourself, but the reality is that a huge number of horses and ponies do travel in a horse box or trailer at some time in their lives, many of them frequently. For instance, your horse will probably have to be moved from its previous owner to the stables where you will keep him. Competitive riders, as well as those who hunt or participate in endurance events, trail riding, polo, polocrosse and so on, need to get their mounts

Above: A well-trained horse will walk straight into the horse box or trailer without any problems.

to the competition venues. Even if you only ride for fun (known as hacking) you may want a change of scenery from time to time − a ride along a nearby beach perhaps. Finally, in the event of illness or injury, the horse may also need to be transported to a veterinary hospital.

Ponies and horses that are imported or exported will travel by air or sea. Even though the travel conditions are different, preparation and care remain much the same as for road travel, which is certainly the most common form of transportation. You can either tow a trailer (confusingly referred to as a horse box in some countries) or you can opt for a larger one-piece horse box (also called a truck, van or float, depending on where you live).

You will, of course, also need suitable travel equipment, including: a head collar, travel boots, tail guard and possibly a poll guard for the head. You may also need a rug for the horse, as well as food and water if the trip is to be a long one.

TRAILERS AND HORSE BOXES

Trailers or horse boxes are manufactured specifically for towing behind suitable domestic vehicles. They usually accommodate from one to three horses, although larger designs that 'gooseneck' onto more powerful vehicles are also available. The most common types are manufactured on a four-wheel chassis and have a small, detachable 'jockey' wheel at the front to support the trailer when it is not attached to the towing vehicle.

There is a wide variety of trailer/horse box designs, most of which have a rear ramp. Some also have a front ramp for offloading. In boxes designed to transport more than a single horse, one or two padded partitions usually divide the space vertically inside. Floors are often covered with rubber or some other non-slip matting, but make sure that you can remove any covering and clean the floor thoroughly. It also needs to be able to dry out to prevent rotting or rusting.

Investigate all the features before you buy your own box. Check its braking system, lights, suspension and all those optional extras that make life so much easier on the road. These include interior lights, saddle racks, tack box, a groom seat, and a water compartment to house your own water container.

Finally, be sure that you have a reliable towing vehicle and a competent driver with the required driver's licence.

Left: A trailer ramp may be covered in rubber matting.

Above: A large truck can be used to transport as many as six horses at once.

Opposite: This luxurious truck has a built-in tack cupboard for added convenience.

Trucks

These are customized vehicles that are manufactured for transporting as many as eight to ten horses at once. Also referred to as 'horse boxes' in many parts of the world, they are more like mini removal vehicles than hitch-on trailers.

Although they are cumbersome, trucks are commonly used as floats for competition or team horses that are travelling some distance to shows. They are probably easier to drive than trailers, although the driver does need to have a special licence. They often provide accommodation for grooms, as well as storage for tack and feed.

Luxury designs incorporate the same kind of facilities for cooking, washing and sleeping as a well-equipped caravan. These are likely to cater for fewer horses, the emphasis being on comfort for the highly competitive rider.

In all instances, running costs are relatively high.

This horse is fitted out with all the equipment necessary to travel: travel boots, tail guard, poll guard and a light stable blanket for warmth. In hot weather, a blanket may not be used.

Travelling equipment

Equipment for transporting a horse is minimal and restricted to items to ensure a safe, injury-free journey.

Horses' legs are particularly vulnerable and should be protected even over a short distance. At very least, fit travel boots or travelling bandages to the lower legs. These should be well padded and properly secured. Ideally, you should also protect the hock and knee. A variety of travel boot designs is available.

Many horses tend to rub the top of their tails on the door of the horse box or trailer in transit. To prevent injury and protect the fleshy dock at the base of the tail, use a tail bandage but do not wrap it too tightly, as this could also injure the tail.

Some sort of sweat rug or blanket is advisable during travel, depending on weather conditions and what the horse is used to. In wet weather, an outdoor blanket will provide protection from wind and rain; after exercise, a sweat sheet or blanket will keep the horse's temperature constant.

For horses that may throw their heads during transportation, or for large horses, a poll guard over the head will give added protection.

A hay net filled with oat hay, straw, lucerne, alfalfa or your horse's usual snack should be provided for the journey, however short it may be. This will distract him and make him more relaxed. If you do not want him to eat within an hour of your arrival – at a show for instance – make a few sacrifices yourself and leave a little earlier.

Avoid leaving any loose objects, including buckets, in the truck or horse box. Anything that can fall about is a potential danger to the horse.

Poll guard

Loading

If you can lead the horse without problems, there is no reason why you should not be able to load him successfully. Start by positioning yourself a few metres from the ramp and then, looking straight ahead and keeping abreast of his shoulder, walk directly up the ramp with him. If he does not follow willingly, do not be tempted to tug or pull. Instead, talk to him quietly in an encouraging tone and try to keep moving forward, however slowly. Try not to turn his head around and start again as you will have lost ground. Keep him facing the horse box and do not turn away. If the horse stops or hesitates, it is sometimes helpful to encourage him by putting one of his front feet on the ramp for him and then pushing gently from behind. Coaxing with feed may also help, although perhaps a sharp tap with a crop may be more effective.

Loading horses can be problematic, particularly if you are inexperienced or unsure of yourself. Horses are sensitive creatures that will take advantage of your insecurity before you even realize it.

A horse is led quietly into a horse box without any problems.

A method that often works for difficult animals is to tie a rope or lead to the side of the box − to the pins that secure the ramp − and ask a helper to bring this around the horse's buttocks to persuade him to move forward. A second lead, tied to the other side, will be even more effective. You will need two helpers and they will cross the two leads behind the horse, preventing him from running or pushing out. Be careful as some horses kick out or rear if they become stressed in this situation.

You should never attempt to ride a horse into the box, but for safety you should use a bridle if the going gets rough. You can also try putting another, more willing horse into the box first. Stand nearby with your horse and lead him in once the first animal is in.

In extreme cases, when a horse consistently refuses to box, possibly because of past trauma, you

TRAVELLING WITH A HORSE

Before you transport a horse yourself, take a ride in a horsebox so you can feel what it is like. In most countries it is unlawful for people to travel in a trailer on public roads, but even a short trip along a farm road or somewhere off the beaten track will give you a good idea of what the horse must endure.

Once on the road with the horse, try to maintain a smooth, steady pace. Avoid sudden braking or accelerating and go around corners slowly. Reduce speed if the road is bumpy. On the open road, build up speed and slow down gradually. Check the box regularly to make sure the horse is safe.

Horses will usually travel happily for four or five hours. If the journey is to take longer, break it to check and water the horses.

Two horses are transported in a horse box or trailer towed by an ordinary domestic vehicle. The gap between the ramp and roof allows a healthy circulation of air.

may need professional assistance. It may take weeks or even months of regularly putting a wary horse in and out of the box at home, with help, before you and the horse can load confidently. Never resort to beating the animal. Wear gloves to avoid rope burns.

When offloading, you or a helper should always untie and then hold the horse securely in the box while someone else opens the ramp and guides him backwards (or forwards if you have a front ramp). Push his hindquarters gently to move him to the centre of the ramp so that he does not slip sideways over the edge and hurt his legs. Some horses run out so you should be ready for this, especially when transporting a horse you do not know.

Left: *Horse boxes (trailers) are lined up at a show.*

BOXING A PROBLEM HORSE

1

The horse has ducked to the side to avoid entering the box.

2

As the trained handler coaxes him forward, he kicks out in resistance.

3

The handler manages to turn him around, but he rears up.

4

The horse does everything to avoid being boxed and leaps over the ramp.

5

Eventually the handler manages to coax him forward slowly.

6

The handler stands quietly with the horse in the box once he is inside.

CHAPTER FIVE

Feeding your Horse

H orses in the wild fend for themselves, grazing constantly. They are selective eaters and generally prefer short, succulent grass. Unlike cattle that use their tongues for grazing, horses use their strong upper lip and front teeth to bite off the grass, then grind the food with their back teeth.

Given enough land with suitable pasture, a horse may be left at grass without supplementing his feed – at least during spring and summer. Since most of our horses live in an unnatural habitat, often in stables, they need their food to be managed for them. Even if some grazing is available, it is usually necessary to provide additional fibre and roughage in the form of straw or hay.

To ensure that the horse's digestive system works properly, he needs small amounts of food, frequently. This is largely because he has a very small stomach and will not be able to digest food properly if too much is given at once.

The overall quantity of food given will depend on the work the horse does, his size and the amount of daily exercise he gets. Food provides energy and, as exercise and work increase, the horse's diet may need to be adjusted to provide additional energy to build up muscle.

Whatever the diet you selected for your horse, he should be fed at the same times each day. He should also have access to plenty of clean water at all times (*see* pages 34 and 43).

NUTRITIONAL NEEDS

All horses need fibre, protein, carbohydrates, fats, certain minerals, trace elements and vitamins, although different types of horses and ponies will thrive on different combinations.

While fibre is found in bulk foods, protein is found in the essential amino acids of most cereals, particularly oats, as well as in most other foodstuffs, including lucerne or alfalfa. Proprietary concentrates and custom-mixed feeds contain a controlled percentage of protein and can usually be relied on to provide what is required for good growth. Although too much protein can be harmful as it overworks the kidneys, lack of protein results in poor condition, lack of appetite and possibly inadequate performance.

THE HORSE'S DIGESTIVE SYSTEM

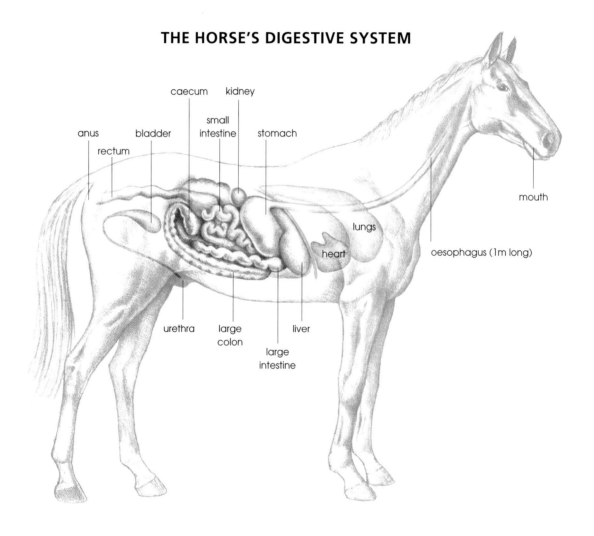

Carbohydrates provide energy and fuel for growth. They are found in various foods, including grasses, cereals and concentrated feeds, as well as in molasses, which is sometimes included in the diet. It is important to have the correct balance of carbohydrate and exercise: too much carbohydrate with too little exercise will result in an overweight horse, while too little carbohydrate will lead to a loss of energy, particularly if you are working the horse hard.

Fat regulates body temperature and keeps the horse's skin and coat healthy. Most concentrates contain a small amount of oil and it is not usually necessary to add more. Too much cod liver oil can be harmful as it unbalances the vitamin and mineral content of the diet. If you decide to add oil to meal, use no more than a tablespoon of cod liver oil a day, or add up to half a cup of vegetable oil to the feed daily. Do not add oil to cubes or pellets.

When it comes to grazing, the grass is always greener on the other side for some horses.

Measure out oil accurately when adding it to feed, and take care not to use too much.

While some minerals and vitamins are present in various types of forage, an unhealthy horse may benefit from supplementation. If the diet is properly controlled, however, vitamins rarely need to be given as a supplement on their own. For instance, although vitamin A may be given to a horse with dry, cracked hooves and a dull coat, it is freely available as carotene in foods such as carrots, grass, maize and lucerne (also known as alfalfa in some parts of the world). Vitamin B, which is needed for a sound nervous system, is seldom lacking if the horse is well fed. Vitamin C, found in grass, is produced in the horse's digestive tract and does not usually need to be supplemented. Vitamin D and the minerals calcium and phosphorous are vital for healthy bone development. Phosphorous is plentiful in cereals, and both molasses and lucerne are high in calcium. Magnesium is also essential for good bone structure and as an enzyme activator, while sulphur is needed to produce enzymes, hormones and amino acids. If a horse's diet is well balanced, the body will produce its own vitamin D by synthesis from the sun's rays. Vitamin E, abundant in sprouting grains, improves the reproductive function of stallions and, to a lesser extent, mares. Vitamin K, also found in sprouting grains and grass, is essential for healthy blood clotting.

Vitamins A, D, E and K are stored in the body fat, while vitamins B and C are water soluble and required daily. With a good, balanced diet, vitamins B and C will be produced naturally by bacterial action in the horse's gut.

FEED

The scientific approach to feeding requires you to detail all the daily requirements exactly in relation to the size of the horse or pony and its exercise regime. Although many breeders and experienced horsemen and women mix their own rations, feed merchants worldwide – many of whom employ qualified animal nutritionists – supply custom mixes in cube, pellet and meal form, which are suitable for different purposes, depending on the energy levels required.

The food chosen, as well as the size of the animal, will determine the quantities to be fed. As a rough guide, the dry weight of the food given each day should be 2.5 per cent of the horse's body weight, provided he is healthy and in good condition. Since weighing a horse is not an easy task, the experts have worked out a system enabling you to estimate weight. To establish his weight in kilograms, measure the horse's girth (around his belly) in metres, to the accuracy of the nearest centimetre. Multiply this by the length from above the elbow of the front leg to the

A hay net keeps fodder dry and contained.

point of the buttock, then multiply by 75. The formula to assess the total weight in pounds involves measuring in inches: multiply the length by the girth measurement, square it, then divide by 300.

Once you know what the horse or pony weighs, you can calculate the total amount of food he should be eating daily. The formula is 2.5 ÷ 100 x weight. Thus, a 12hh pony weighing 300kg (660 lb) will eat about 7.5kg (16 ½ lb) of food each day, while a 16.2hh horse weighing double this will have an approximate capacity of 15kg (33 lb).

Of course, this does not tell you what the foodstuffs should consist of, but it should generally be a combination of types. Apart from anything else, some horses require more energy-giving foods than others. Climatic and living conditions also come into play, since horses can use up to 30 per cent of their body weight maintaining body temperature.

ESTIMATING A HORSE'S WEIGHT

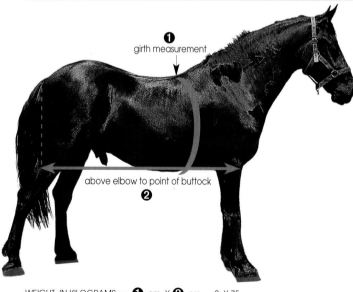

WEIGHT IN KILOGRAMS: = ❶ cm X ❷ cm = ? X 75

WEIGHT IN POUNDS : = ❶ in. X ❷ in. = ?. ?² ÷ 300

DAILY FOOD INTAKE: 2.5 ÷ 100 X weight

As a broad guide, if the pony is at grass and is ridden for no more than an hour a day – mostly walking and trotting – he can happily survive on grass and/or hay alone. If he does more active work – cantering, jumping or going to gymkhana games, for instance – you need to substitute 15 per cent of the bulk foods with concentrates (1kg or 2¼ lb of cubes or meal divided into two or three meals). A 12hh pony is unlikely to be doing more strenuous work. A 16.2hh horse, however, may be in training for horse trials, long-distance endurance riding, hunting or even polo, in which case 45 to 55 per cent of the bulk feed should take the form of concentrates.

Even if the horse is not being worked much, he may be fed up to 15 per cent of his food (2.25kg or 5 lb) in concentrates. If the horse is in light work – an hour's riding a day – this can be increased to 25 per cent (3.75kg or 8 lb). If he is competing at jumping or dressage shows, it should be increased to one-third of the diet (5kg or 11 lb divided into three or four feeds a day). If in doubt, consult an expert.

Bulk foods and fodder

Bulk foods (including grass) and fodder (including straw and hay) provide horses with roughage and some nourishment and are an essential element of any equine diet. These foodstuffs should generally be given before feeding concentrates, to prevent the horse from guzzling.

Grass is first prize for a horse, although the quality varies depending on what occurs naturally or what has been planted. If he cannot graze for some reason such as ill health or injury, but you have access to fresh-cut grass, fill a large sack and feed immediately. Cut the grass as long as possible and do not leave it standing for any length of time as it can overheat, which could cause colic. Since most lawns are treated with herbicides, never feed lawn mowings.

There are different types of *hay*, depending on the kind of grass utilized and the region in which you live. In the United Kingdom, for instance, soft meadow hay is considered ideal for ponies as it contains a variety of grasses, as well as clover and herbs. Seed hay is

Horses should be fed fodder in the stable, even if they are put out to grass during the day.

Teff   *Straw*   *Lucerne/alfalfa*   *Oat hay*

cultivated and may also contain a mixture of grasses. It is said to be more nutritious than meadow hay and more suitable for competition horses. Teff grass or rye-grass hay, which is reasonably high in protein but low in minerals, may also be used as fodder.

Hay should be made in dry, sunny weather, when the grass has flowered but before it goes to seed. It should not be fed to horses or ponies until it is at least two months old. If it is fed too soon, it can cause colic; if it is kept too long, its nutritional quality deteriorates.

In some parts of the world, *haylage* (or hayage) is fed for roughage. A mixture of grass and other green crops, it is sold bagged under various brand names. It is damper than normal hay and is often fed to animals with allergies. It is also useful when good quality hay is scarce. Once the bag has been opened, it should be used immediately as it tends to become mouldy within a few days. Feed according to the manufacturer's instructions.

Soaked hay may also be fed to horses that are allergic to the spores found in hay. Put the hay in the hay net before soaking in a bucket of clean water or by hosing. Allow it to drain before feeding. If the hay net is not finished that day, discard the damp hay.

Oat hay is a by-product of oats and, like all hays, should be made in dry, sunny weather. In some countries, the tops of oat plants are cut, together with the seeds and juicy stalks, to make what is known as oat hay. The coarser, bottom stalks are then cut, dried and sold as straw. This may also be fed to horses, especially fat, little ponies, but does not have as much nourishment and is not as tasty.

Barley and wheat straws are not suitable as feed.

Lucerne, known as alfalfa in the United States and other parts of the world, is a clover-type plant grown and processed in the same way as hay. It has a high nutritional value with lots of protein and essential amino acids, high calcium content and very little phosphorous. If it is added to the horse's diet, less concentrate should be fed. Although it does not affect the behaviour of all horses, lucerne or alfalfa can make some of them 'hot' (unduly excited when ridden).

All fodder should be sweet-smelling and free from dust or mildew. If it smells musty it was probably baled damp and should be discarded.

Below: Oat hay makes a tasty snack at any time.

FEEDING INGREDIENTS

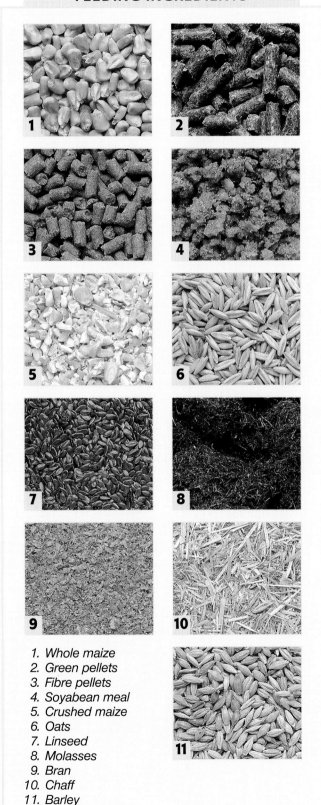

1. Whole maize
2. Green pellets
3. Fibre pellets
4. Soyabean meal
5. Crushed maize
6. Oats
7. Linseed
8. Molasses
9. Bran
10. Chaff
11. Barley

Cereals

Cereals, particularly oats and bran, are often included in the horse's diet.

Oats are considered to be the best source of energy for horses, although they are a 'heating' food and should generally not be given to high-spirited horses or excitable ponies as it makes them too energetic and difficult to ride. Oats may be fed whole if soaked for about 12 hours beforehand, or added rolled or crushed. Traditionally, oats were mixed with barley or bran and chopped hay or straw – referred to as chaff or chop. Today, many horse owners prefer to feed manufactured concentrates that contain oats.

Barley may be used rolled or crushed, but should never be fed whole unless it has been soaked and thoroughly boiled for a couple of hours. Mixed with bran it makes a good mash that is easily digestible. Flaked barley is easier to digest than rolled or crushed barley and is sometimes substituted for oats if the horse gets too 'hot'. It is generally a better option for ponies.

Flaked or crushed maize (corn) is added to some feeds to add variety. Since it is fattening and causes most horses to become 'hot', it should be used only in small quantities. If whole maize is used, it should be soaked for 24 hours.

Bran – from wheat and sometimes from oats – is often used to bulk up food and aid digestion. Fed damp, it acts as a mild laxative. Sick horses are sometimes fed a warm wheaten bran mash made by pouring boiling water over the bran. For 1kg (2 lb) of bran, add a tablespoon of salt or Epsom salts and a little linseed jelly to make it more palatable. Traditionally fed to horses once a week in winter to improve the coat, linseed jelly is made with about 60g (2oz) of the seed covered with about 1.7 litres (3pt) of water and soaked for 24 hours to soften before boiling. It is essential to simmer until all the seeds have split, as uncooked or partially cooked seeds can be toxic. Mix in with the evening feed while the 'jelly' is still warm.

Concentrates

Available as cubes, pellets or nuts, or as coarse meal mixes, concentrates are the preferred equine option for many horse owners today. The ingredients of both mixes and cubes are carefully planned by trained nutritionists and made up in strictly supervised factory conditions. Energy levels, as well as suitability for specific horses, are usually stated on the label. In some countries, concentrates are referred to as a per centage, which relates directly to the protein levels. For instance, 10 per cent is suitable for most riding horses, and 14–16 per cent for racehorses. Alternatively, they may be referred to by the purpose for which they have been prepared, for example, for horse and pony, Warmblood, stud, and so on.

The same content is usually available in both pelleted and loose-mix forms. Some horse owners believe their animals get bored eating pellets and prefer mixes because you can see what is in them.

The processed content usually includes traditional ingredients like oats, bran, maize, etc, sometimes with the addition of soya, plant oils, vitamins, minerals and various other additives. Grains may be steam flaked, a process similar to microwaving, or extruded to break down the starch structure. Unlike traditional cereal mixes, new-generation feeds that come in a 'slow-release' form are based on high-energy fibres rather than high-energy starches. This improves stamina and is ideal for competitive, high-performance horses.

Horses love apples; and children love to feed them. This Appaloosa (with leopard spots to match the dalmations') is no exception.

A coarse meal mix, ready to eat

When buying concentrates, make sure you buy a reputable brand so that you can be reasonably sure the product will be consistent. Unfortunately, if certain ingredients are in short supply, consistency can become a problem.

When feeding concentrates, always follow the manufacturer's instructions and do not overfeed. You may think you are giving too little, particularly when feeding cubes, but in this instance it is safer to feed too little than too much.

Additives

Various additives and supplements are often included in the feed, even when custom-mixed brands are being fed. Familiarize yourself with the ingredients of any supplement you are planning to give your horse, ensuring these will not react with supplements that may have been added to ready-mixed feeds and concentrates. When in doubt, consult an animal nutritionist or veterinarian.

Electrolytes or tissue salts, such as sodium, chlorine and potassium, are essential for the regulation of all athletes' body fluids, and this applies to horses as well. In hot-climate countries, in warm weather and after strenuous exercise or training for events like long-distance endurance riding, three-day eventing and polo, electrolytes should be supplemented. Salt (sodium chloride) is easy to add to the diet; you can either add a big pinch to each meal or provide the horse with a salt lick, available from tack shops and some feed merchants. Fixed to the stable wall, these are convenient and practical, but are not favoured by all horses. Potassium, found in the low herbal growth of some pastures, may be supplemented with cider vinegar. Alternatively, a proprietary electrolyte mixture may be given.

Salt and mineral lick blocks are available in several flavours, sizes and shapes.

Molasses, a by-product of sugar cane, has a high nutritional value and is regarded as a treat by many horses. In fact, many horse owners use a handful of molasses mixed with worm mixtures and medicines to make them easier to feed to their horses. While this is acceptable, molasses should never be mixed with inferior food simply to make the horse eat. In its liquid form, molasses looks like black treacle; when sold in meal form, it is slightly sticky to the touch and looks a bit like coarse potting soil.

Vegetables

Vegetables and some fruits may be fed to horses and ponies, the most universally popular being carrots (which are often available in bulk) and apples. Other root vegetables, such as turnips, beetroots, parsnips and swedes, are also highly nutritious, although it may take a while for the horse to adapt to their taste. Root vegetables may be eaten safely in reasonably large quantities (as much as 1kg or 2 lb a day). Apples are particularly popular because they are sweet and tasty, but take care not to feed too many as they can cause colic if eaten in large quantities.

FEEDING YOUR HORSE

The first step is to establish a routine. Horses are creatures of habit and will anticipate meal times according to the clock. It is ideal to feed three or four times a day, although this is not always practical, particularly if you are working and do not have the assistance of a groom. You need to feed at least every morning and every evening, and to ensure that the horse has grass to graze and/or some other kind of bulk food in a hay net or manger if he is stabled, or in a hay net or feeding bin if he is in the paddock.

Mix the feed in a suitable feed container before taking it to the horse. Keep a suitable scoop in the feed room, having established what each scoop weighs and how many scoops you should give. Mix everything together and moisten it slightly if giving dry foods, particularly if fine bran is included. Make sure the horse has drunk water before you feed, then top up all water buckets or troughs in the stable and paddock before you leave.

Never feed a horse directly before or after exercise. Wait at least an hour before riding, and after a ride, cool the horse down by walking for a short while. Then give him water and a hay net and wait until his pulse and respiration are back to normal and he stops sweating – feel under the chest to ensure he is no longer hot before feeding him.

FOOD STORAGE

Ideally, you need a separate feed room large enough to store all forms of forage: concentrates, any individual cereals used, supplements and a reasonable supply of fodder – hay, lucerne or alfalfa, and so on. Fodder should be stacked away from the floor on pallets to keep it dry. The room must be dry, cool and clean and should house bins, drums and any other suitable containers that can be securely closed.

Left: Oat hay and lucerne/alfalfa bales are neatly stacked in a feed room.

Horses should be encouraged to drink water before they are fed.

You need several bins that can be sealed so you can decant different types of feed. It is important to finish old feed before decanting new provisions. Moulded plastic is a good material, unlike most paper or hessian bags, which are easily chewed through by rodents. But however careful and clean you are, rats and mice are attracted to hay, straw and lucerne, which is why so many cats are gainfully employed at stables all over the world.

If a horse gets into the feed room, ensure he cannot tip the bins over or knock off the lids. A horse can get a fatal dose of colic if he overeats – and this has been known to happen to horses that have managed to enter a feed room.

Right: *Feed is safely stored in a big bin and barrels.*

Your Horse's Health

A healthy horse is a happy horse – a fact that usually helps any observant horse owner to identify illness or sudden injury. It should not take long to familiarize yourself with your horse's normal behaviour and demeanour, after which you should be able to identify any abnormal signs.

Of course, it helps to have a thorough knowledge of normal equine behaviour and a perception of what can go wrong. For instance, a healthy horse rolls for pleasure whereas a horse with colic rolls in agony; and while all horses rest their hind legs when standing perfectly relaxed in the paddock or stable, it may indicate injury when a horse rests his front leg.

Take every possible precaution to keep your horse healthy – not only practising good stable management, but ensuring he receives routine veterinary treatments, including regular deworming, teeth floating and all the necessary vaccinations.

Finally, you need to know what to do in an emergency and how to determine when it is necessary or advisable to call in a veterinary surgeon or other qualified practitioner.

PROFESSIONAL ASSISTANCE

All horse owners require the assistance of a veterinarian at some stage, even if the horse is perfectly healthy. Although all vets receive the same basic training, some specialize in horses, so even if your local vet normally looks after your dogs and cats, he or she may not be the best person to care for your pony or horse. Personal recommendation is a good way to find a suitable vet. Ideally, you want someone reasonably close to the stables; not only do most vets charge for travelling, but he or she will also be able to get to you more quickly in an emergency. Nonetheless, vets do sometimes make visits to specific areas on certain days and, provided you use their services then, you will not be charged for transport.

Recently, a growing number of practitioners trained in fields such as physiotherapy, homeopathy, chiropractic and acupuncture have turned their skills to the care of horses. Others specialize in equine dentistry. In an emergency, always contact a vet first. If you want to use other practitioners, you should ideally have your vet's support. If not, try to find one who will accept your desire to use alternative remedies.

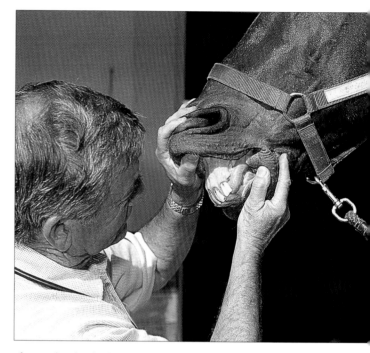

A vet checks for healthy gums and teeth.

THE HEALTHY HORSE

The general attitude of any horse gives a good indication of his wellbeing. He should be alert and attentive all the time, and interested in things happening around him. His eyes should be bright and clear without any form of discharge, and the mucus membrane under the lids should be a salmon-pink colour rather than white, yellow or red. The insides of his nostrils, as well as the lips and gums, should also be salmon-pink.

If his head is hung low, chances are he is feeling poorly. His coat should shine, especially after he has been groomed. A dry coat, tight skin or evidence of sores, lumps and bald spots are reliable indications of poor health. Check his legs regularly, particularly after hard workouts and competitions. If they become puffy or swollen, or if you can feel heat, take immediate action. Unless you are certain of the cause and know what treatment is necessary, call the vet.

Check your horse's droppings daily. They should be green to golden-brown in colour, firm and moist, and should crumble when they hit the ground. Horses

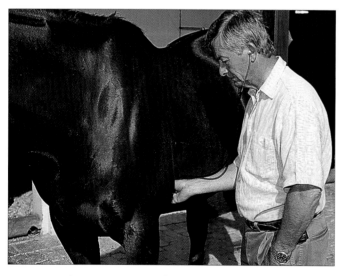

A vet cuses a stethoscope to check the pulse of a horse. Between 36 and 42 beats per minute when at rest is normal.

pass anything from eight to 15 piles a day. If there are very few, he may be constipated; if there are none at all, something more serious may be wrong. If droppings are dry or slimy, smell offensive or contain blood, mucus or undigested food, you should be concerned. Dark urine is another

Healthy droppings

sign the horse is not well. Inability to pass urine or straining when urinating could indicate an obstruction; excessive urinating is also abnormal.

Loss of appetite and a refusal to drink water are sure indications that something is wrong.

Learn how to establish whether temperature, respiration and pulse are normal, and be aware that these will change during exercise and training.

Temperature is always a fair indication of health or sickness. Although you can use an ordinary thermometer, a veterinary thermometer is preferable. Lubricate the bulb end with petroleum jelly, lift the tail and insert it into the rectum. Remember to stand to the side of the hindquarters and, if you sense the horse may kick, get a helper to pick up one of the front legs. Hold the thermometer firmly, pressing it against the wall of the rectum for one or two minutes. Normal temperature is between 37.2°C and 38.3°C (99–101°F). If it is not within these limits, call the vet.

Pulse rates of horses should be between 36 to 42 beats per minute when at rest. The easiest places to detect the pulse are at the artery just behind the elbow, under the jaw where there is a facial artery, or near the jugular vein in the neck. The most accurate way of taking the pulse is to use a stethoscope and the second hand of a watch to assess the number of beats per minute. Alternatively, count the pulse for ten seconds and multiply by six to calculate the pulse rate per minute.

During exercise, the pulse or heart rate will increase dramatically. For instance, a horse walking actively will have a pulse rate of 60–70 beats a minute; after a short canter workout, it will rise to as much as 150 beats per minute. If the horse is at rest and his pulse is high, he may be in pain, have a fever, or simply be frightened.

Respiration rate refers to the number of breaths a horse takes every minute. When he is at rest, he should breathe in and out eight to 18 times – each in-and-out motion counting as one breath. To establish your horse's respiration rate, watch the rise and fall of the flanks or put your hand against his nostrils to feel the air on your hand.

Like pulse rates, respiration rates increase during exercise and when a horse is ill or frightened.

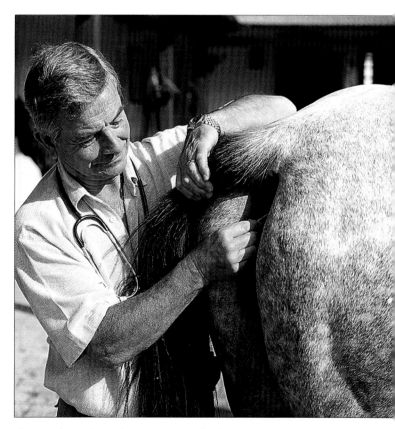

A vet takes a horse's temperature in the rectum using an equine thermometer.

PREVENTING ILL HEALTH

When it comes to the health of your horse, sensible preventative measures save not only heartache but also money in the long run. It stands to reason that horses that are not vaccinated against equine influenza (flu) and dewormed regularly are more likely to get sick than horses enjoying the benefit of this routine attention.

Parasites

Internal parasites can cause major problems if neglected. In extreme cases, they can cause severe suffering and even death. Precautionary measures should be two-fold. The first step is to ensure that droppings are regularly picked up and removed from stables and paddocks. Fields and paddocks should also be rotated in order to ensure healthy grazing (*see* page 34).

Below: An intravenous injection should be administered by a qualified veterinarian.

Ensure that the horse is dewormed regularly to keep these harmful parasites to a minimum. There are various 'wormer' brands, which are available in either paste or powder format. To achieve maximum results, avoid using any one type or brand regularly. This will prevent worms from building up immunity. Whichever type you use, it is essential to give the correct amount. This is calculated by weight (*see* page 102). Too little will be ineffective, while too much may lead to immunity and possibly even a sick horse. Make sure that you follow the manufacturer's instructions carefully and that you liaise with your vet for advice.

Of several worms that infect horses, the worst is the large red worm. This parasite lives in the gut or on the walls of the intestines and can cause considerable internal damage. Symptoms of infestation include loss of weight, a dull coat and diarrhoea.

Small red worms cause massive inflammation and ulceration of the horse's large intestinal wall, anaemia and constipation, as well as digestive problems.

Roundworms are generally less of a problem, although they are often very long and infestation can be extensive. However, they can be a major problem in foals and young horses.

Tapeworms sometimes occur and need to be treated, but are not common in horses.

Bot eggs, laid by the troublesome gadfly, are tiny and difficult to remove. A special bot knife (*see* page 66) should be used to scrape them off.

External parasites can also be harmful, particularly ticks and lice. They are relatively easy to control with proprietary treatments, powders, shampoos and sprays, but can be a problem if neglected. Ask a vet for advice if you are unsure what to use or how often to treat.

Vaccination

Vaccination requirements vary from country to country, so ensure you know which are required and when. Details will be recorded on a certificate or in the horse's passport to ensure they are carried out regularly, as required.

Some of the most common vaccinations include equine flu, tetanus and, in parts of Africa, African horse sickness. Most vaccinations are given annually, when the horse is not in work.

- *Tetanus* is a serious disease caused by bacteria in the soil that can infect wounds. It is often fatal. If a horse that has not been vaccinated against tetanus is wounded, call the vet immediately – even a minor cut could lead to tetanus. Symptoms include stiffness and reluctance to move, overreaction to noise and loss of appetite. An initial course of injections, often combined with a flu vaccination, is followed by an annual booster.

- *Botulism* is a fatal toxin from feed contaminated by dead mice, rats, birds, and so on. Its effects are similar to tetanus.

- *Equine influenza* is a virus similar to the one that attacks humans. It is highly infectious and can be severe. In some countries, regular vaccinations against equine flu are mandatory, especially for competition and racehorses. Even if not compulsory, vaccination is advisable. There are different strains that can lead to breakdown in immunity. Although the vaccination cannot guarantee the horse will never get flu, symptoms will generally be milder. Like the tetanus vaccine, flu vaccines involve primary vaccinations followed by boosters. Your vet will advise.

- *Rhinopneumonitis* vaccinations are commonly given to horses in the United States and some

A nasal discharge could be serious. Check with your vet to ascertain its cause.

parts of the United Kingdom. A contagious viral infection that causes colds in young horses, it also leads to abortion in pregnant mares. Young horses go off their feed, cough, have a nasal discharge and develop a fever. Unfortunately, pregnant mares may show no symptoms at all. Sick horses should be isolated and treated by a vet, usually with antibiotics. The immune response of the vaccine is short-lived, so boosters are usually given quarterly.

- *Equine encephalomyelitis* is a serious viral disease for which there is no known treatment. It is restricted to the Americas, and in the United States horses travelling to competitions must be vaccinated against it annually. Initial symptoms include mild loss of appetite, low fever, depression and possible hypersensitivity to external stimuli. As the disease worsens, animals may appear blind or experience tremors, which may lead to paralysis. It is transmitted

Swollen glands such as these are usually a sign that a horse is unwell and needs the attention of a vet.

COMMON AILMENTS

Ponies and horses are also prone to numerous common ailments. While good stable management will keep these to a minimum, you should know what steps to take if they occur. When in doubt, call the vet.

Coughs and colds

These are common in horses. An equine cold is similar to a human one, often starting with a rise in temperature and a runny nose. Coughs frequently accompany colds but may simply be due to an allergy. In the event of infection, take the horse off work and, if necessary, keep him in the stable. The vet will advise and prescribe any necessary medication.

by insects, especially mosquitoes, and thought to be spread by wild birds. It is considered a significant public health issue as human infection can occur, usually resulting in brain damage or death. There are several strains, and vaccines are available for Western and Eastern encephalomyelitis.

- *African horse sickness* has been known to kill in epidemic proportions. A virus transmitted by midges, it is most common in hot, rainy conditions. Symptoms include high fever, swollen eyelids, heavy breathing and foaming at the nostrils. Animals can be protected by vaccination. During an outbreak, owners are advised to make frequent use of insect repellents and to stable their horses from late afternoon until mid-morning. Over the years there have been numerous embargoes on the movement of horses in parts of southern Africa as well as on the export of horses from that part of the world. There are various different strains of the disease and vaccinations are not 100 per cent effective.

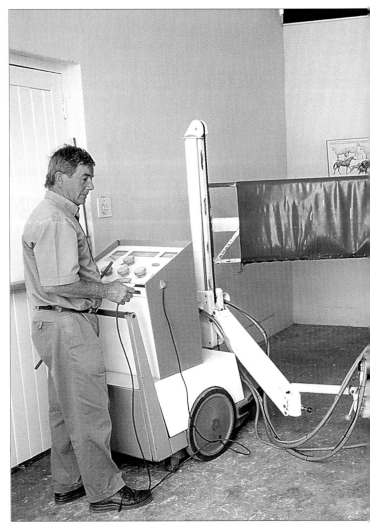

Lameness

This term refers to any horse or pony that is not 100 per cent sound. It may be due to an injured or strained tendon or a bruised sole after the animal has stepped on a stone. It may also be because the saddle does not fit correctly and the muscles in his back are sore. A horse may even go lame because he is not fit enough for the work he is being asked to do or because of incorrect shoeing.

It is usually obvious: the horse shifts his weight off the sore leg and may limp, appearing unbalanced. If you think your horse is lame, trot him out and ask your instructor or other experienced person to check his paces. Once you identify which limb is lame, feel for heat or swelling and check for wounds. If there is nothing obvious, an X-ray may be necessary. It is advisable to call a vet to decide on treatment.

Saddle and bridle sores

These are usually caused by ill-fitting or dirty tack that rubs the coat and causes swelling or rawness. The girth can also rub away the hair and cause raw, bleeding sores. These conditions often occur because of ignorance and deteriorate because of neglect. Zinc cream may be used to heal the sores: persist twice a day until they dry out and heal. In severe cases, call the vet and rest the horse.

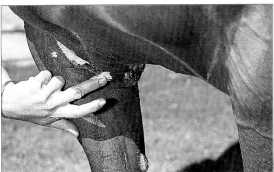

Above: An antibacterial cream is applied to a deep wound to prevent infection.

Left: A horse has his leg X-rayed to ascertain whether or not there is evidence of injury.

Thrush

A bacterial infection that affects the frog of the horse's foot, thrush is often due to poor stable management, for example: wet, dirty stables; muddy paddocks; and feet that have not been properly cleaned or regularly attended to by the farrier. The foot of a horse with thrush smells and must be thoroughly cleaned, dried and treated with iodine, Stockholm tar or a suitable proprietary dressing.

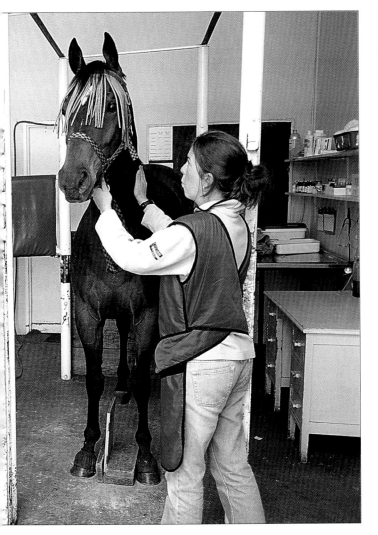

Skin conditions

- *Sweet itch* is an allergic condition caused by insect bites – probably a species of sandfly. The horse rubs himself against trees or paddock fencing to relieve the itch. It is most common along the mane and tail and results in ugly, inflamed patches. Use sweet itch lotion to relieve the sores, and strong fly repellent to keep the insects away.
- *Ringworm* is an infectious fungal condition not unlike human ringworm. It results in small raised patches that often become raw. Infected horses should be treated with proprietary lotions and their bedding burnt. Prevent its spread by using separate brushes and tack, and isolate a horse with ringworm to prevent the spread of infection.
- *Contagious acne* looks a bit like ringworm, with small, round inflamed areas appearing on the coat, usually on the girth or saddle area. Like ringworm, it is infectious. It can be treated successfully with iodine-type products.

Mud fever

Mud fever and cracked heels are caused by a bacterial infection of the skin around heel and pastern. The feet become sore and the legs swollen, with a yellow discharge from the skin. Avoid it by good cleaning, removing mud regularly and keeping the feet dry. Trimming the heel feathers prevents accumulation of mud.

Laminitis

A very serious condition or syndrome, laminitis requires prompt treatment. Affecting ponies more often than horses, it is often caused by overfeeding. It results in inflammation and swelling of the feet, especially the front feet. Cold hosing of the feet will give temporary relief, but it is essential to call the vet. Badly conformed feet are more prone to the disease than those that are well conformed. A pony with laminitis should not be ridden until the condition has cleared.

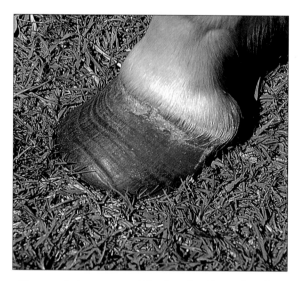

Abnormal rings around the hoof wall are the visible effects of severe laminitis.

Strangles

A highly contagious disease aggravated by cold, wet weather, strangles is caused by the *Streptococcus equi* bacterium. Symptoms include a high fever, loss of appetite, yellow nasal discharge and a moist cough. The horse may also have difficulty in swallowing and the lymph glands usually swell dramatically. Isolate sick animals and call the vet timeously. Strangles spreads rapidly and can be lethal in yards housing large numbers of horses.

Left: Mud fever can be unsightly and painful.

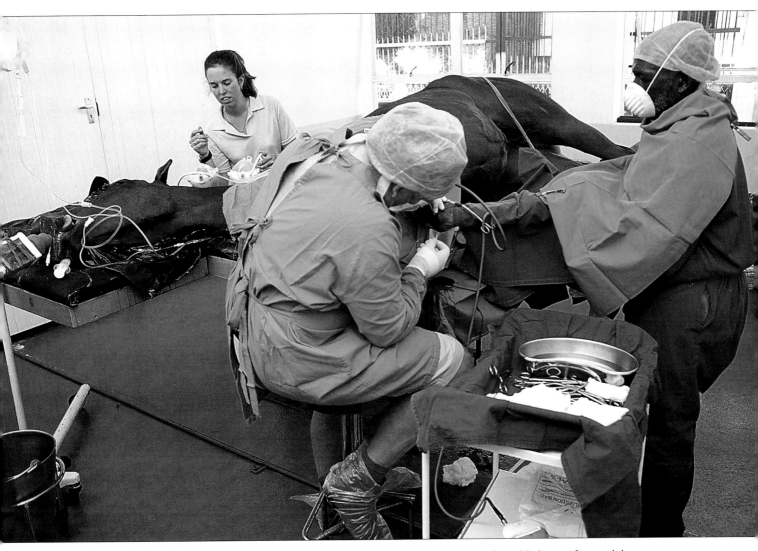

When surgery is necessary, as with this horse having bone chips removed from his knee after an injury, the animal will need to be anaesthetized in a properly equipped veterinary surgery.

Biliary (piroplasmosis)

This is a parasite of red blood cells in horses, transmitted by ticks. Symptoms include loss of appetite, depression and fever. The mucus membranes become yellow and jaundiced, and the horse is often constipated. It is a serious disease and can be fatal. If you suspect it, call the vet immediately.

Colic

Knowing the symptoms of colic is crucial as it can be fatal. In layman's terms, it may be indigestion, a blockage or even a twisted section of bowel or gut, which may even lead to a severe stomachache that makes the horse roll in pain. Unlike the pleasurable rolling horses normally do, a horse with colic tends to thrash around. Since it comes in spasms, he may appear to be normal in between. If you suspect colic, the traditional practice is to keep the horse walking to prevent rolling, though this can tire him. The danger is that a horse can twist his gut while he writhes around. Call the vet immediately for an accurate diagnosis and treatment. Although colic can be treated with drugs, surgery is sometimes needed. Fast action is required.

EQUINE FIRST AID KIT

Be prepared for any emergency. Keep a first-aid kit at the stables and always take the essential items with you when travelling or competing. Check the expiry date of all medicines, and in the event of serious injury or illness, call the vet. Make sure you have:

- a selection of bandages, plus tape and pins
- gamgee (cotton encased in gauze)

- cotton wool and gauze
- a cold treatment pack
- salt (or saline water)
- antiseptic

- wound spray or cream
- antibiotic powder
- sharp scissors
- thermometer

- syringe
- Epsom salts
- petroleum jelly
- leg poultices and cooling agents

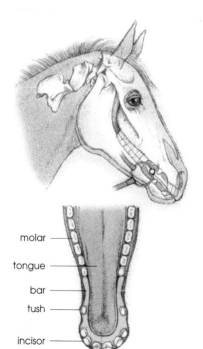

molar
tongue
bar
tush
incisor

TEETH

Like humans, horses have two sets of teeth in a lifetime. By looking at the teeth you can estimate a horse's age, though you need a trained eye and an understanding of the structure of the teeth.

Most horses start losing their baby 'milk' teeth at about two-and-a-half years old. By the time they are four, they have most of their permanent teeth, though the canines usually only erupt when they are about five, at which point they have what is referred to as 'a full mouth'.

Unlike human teeth, the horse's teeth continue to grow throughout his life. Even though they are worn down when he chews and grinds his food, they need to be rasped or floated every six to 12 months with a

HOW TEETH AGE

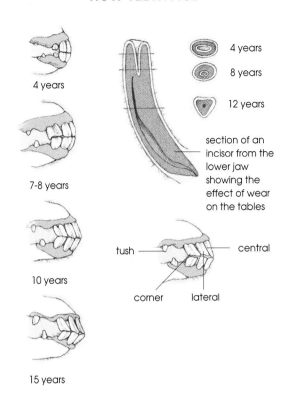

4 years

7-8 years

10 years

15 years

4 years

8 years

12 years

section of an incisor from the lower jaw showing the effect of wear on the tables

tush — central

corner   lateral

A vet needs help to keep a horse's mouth open and the head still while he rasps the teeth.

long-handled rasp – a task done by a vet or equine dentist. The molars get very sharp edges over time and can cut the tongue and insides of the cheeks if this is not done.

Equine dentists and some vets have more specialized tools that enable them to balance, float and rectify problems, including sharp hooks and waves, more effectively. The horse may need to be tranquillized, in which case a vet will have to be present.

Horses and ponies also experience abnormalities of tooth eruption, so it is essential to check regularly that the mouth is developing naturally, particularly in young animals. If the eruption of the small underdeveloped teeth just in front of the upper molars, known as wolf teeth, coincides with a reluctance to accept the bit or uncharacteristic throwing of the horse's head, consider having them removed to relieve pressure and discomfort.

OLD AGE

Although not old, a horse over 10 years is referred to as 'aged' as it becomes more difficult to assess his age accurately from his teeth. However, horses generally live much longer.

As he ages, his physical condition may deteriorate. Once he is no longer ridden, muscle tone is reduced and the neck loses strength. Sunken hollows form around the eyes, the back becomes hollow and the withers appear more pronounced. Geriatric horses walk more slowly and carefully and may seem to be stiff.

A horse older than 15 years should be checked by the vet at least once a year. Also check his teeth regularly as they are likely to break and eventually fall out. This will affect the way he chews and could impede digestion and lead to colic. As they age, horses lose their natural ability to regulate and maintain body temperature, so they should be properly rugged and given adequate protection in bad weather.

If you decide to retire your horse to a farm where he can live out his life in a well-grassed field, make sure regular veterinary attention is available and that there is sufficient shelter and grazing. Never abandon an old horse in a paddock: now, more than ever, he needs attention and companionship.

FEI National Federations

Fédération Equestre Internationale (FEI)
PO Box 157, 1000 Lausanne 5
Switzerland
Tel: + 41 21 310-4747
Fax: + 41 21 310-4760
http://www.horsesport.org
has 128 member countries, including:

AUSTRALIA
Equestrian Federation of Australia
Level 2, 196 Greenhill Rd, Eastwood
SA 5063
Tel: + 61 88 357-0077
Fax: + 61 88 357-0091
email: info@efanational.com

AUSTRIA
Bundesfachverband für Reiten und
Fahren in Österreich
Geiselbergstrasse 26-32/512, Wien 1110
Tel: + 43 1 749-9261
Fax: + 43 1 749-9291
email: office@fena.at

BELGIUM
Fédération Royale Belge des Sports
Equestres
Avenue Houba de Strooper 156
Bruxelles 1020
Tel: + 32 2 478-5056
Fax: + 32 2 478-1126
email: info@equibel.be

CANADA
Equine Canada
2460 Lancaster Road, Suite 200
Ottawa, Ontario KIB 455
Tel: + 1 613 248-3433
Fax: + 1 613 248-3484
email: dadams@equestrian.ca

FRANCE
Fédération Française d'Equitation
Immeuble le Quintet, Bâtiment E 81/83
Avenue E. Valliant, Boulogna, Billancourt
92517 Cedex
Tel: + 33 1 5817-5817
Fax: + 33 1 5817-5853
email: dtnadj@ffe.com

GERMANY
Deutsche Reiterliche Vereinigung
PO Box 110265, Warendorf 48231
Tel: + 49 2581 6-3620
Fax: + 49 2581 6-2144
email: fn@fn-dokr.de

IRELAND
Equestrian Federation of Ireland
Ashton House
Castleknock, Dublin 1515
Tel: + 353 1 868-8222
Fax: + 353 1 882-3782
email: efi@horsesport.ie

ITALY
Italian Equestrian Federation
Viale Tiziano 74-76, 00196 Rome
Tel: + 39 6 3685-8105
Fax: + 39 6 323-3772
email: fise@fise.it

NETHERLANDS
Stichting Nederlandse Hippische
Sportbond
PO Box 3040, Ca Ermelo 3850
Tel: + 31 577 40-8200
Fax: + 31 577 40-1725
email: info@nhs.nl

NEW ZEALAND
New Zealand Equestrian Federation
PO Box 6146, Te Aro, Wellington 6035
Tel: + 64 4 801-6449
Fax: + 64 4 801-7701
email: nzef@nzequestrian.org.nz

NORWAY
Norges Rytterforbund
Serviceboks 1 u.s.
Sognsveien 75, Oslo 0840
Tel: + 47 21 02-9650
Fax: + 47 21 02-9651
email: nryf@rytter.no

PORTUGAL
Federaçao Equestre Portuguesa
Avenida Manuel da Maia No. 26
4eme Droite, Lisbon 1000-201

Tel: + 351 21 847-8774
Fax: + 351 21 847-4582
email: secgeral@fep.pt

SOUTH AFRICA
SA National Equestrian Federation
PO Box 30875, Kyalami, 1684 Gauteng
Tel: + 27 11 468-3236
Fax: + 27 11 468-3238
email: sanef@iafrica.com

SPAIN
Real Federaçion Hipica Espanola
C/Ayala No. 6, 6° drcha, Madrid 28001
Tel: + 34 91 436-4200
Fax: + 34 91 575-0770
email: rfhe@rfhe.com

SWEDEN
Svenska Ridsportförbundet
Ridsportens Hus, Strömsholm
Kolback 73040
Tel: + 46 220 4-5600
Fax: + 46 220 4-5670
email: kansliet@ridsport.se

SWITZERLAND
Fédération Suisse des Sports Equestres
H Case Postale 726, 3000 Berne 22
Tel: + 41 31 335-4343
Fax: + 41 31 335-4357/8
email: vst@svps-fsse.ch

UNITED KINGDOM
British Equestrian Federation
National Agricultural Centre
Stoneleigh Park, Kenilworth
Warwickshire, Warcs CV8 2RH
Tel: + 44 24 7669-8871
Fax: + 44 24 7669-6484
email: info@bef.co.uk

UNITED STATES OF AMERICA
USA Equestrian Inc.
4047 Iron Works Parkway
Lexington 40511-8483KY
Tel: + 1 859 258-2472
Fax: + 1 859 253-1968
email: sfrank@equestrian.org

Further Reading

Baird, Eric. (1977). *Horse Care*. London: Macdonald and Jane's.

Belton, Christina (translator). (1997). *The Principles of Riding: The Official Instruction Handbook of the German National Equestrian Federation – Part 1*. Addington, Great Britain: Kenilworth Press.

Bird, Catherine. (2002). *A Healthy Horse the Natural Way*. Sydney: New Holland Publishers.

Callery, Emma (ed). (1994). *The New Rider's Companion*. London: The Apple Press.

Cooper, Barbara. (2000). *The Manual of Horsemanship*. London: The Pony Club.

Culshaw, Doris. (1995). *Bits, Bridles & Saddles*. London: B. T. Batsford.

Draper, Judith. (1999). *Illustrated Encyclopaedia: Horse Breeds of the World*. London: Sebastian Kelly.

Edwards, Elwyn Hartley (ed). (1977). *Encyclopaedia of the Horse*. London: Octopus Books.

Edwards, Elwyn Hartley. (2000). *The New Encyclopaedia of the Horse*. London: Dorling Kindersley.

Faurie, Bernadette. (2000). *The Horse Riding & Care Handbook*. London: New Holland Publishers.

Fitchet, Peter. (1991). *Horse Health Care*. Johannesburg: Delta Books.

Green, Carol. (1990). *Tack Explained*. London: Ward Lock.

Hawcroft, Tim. (1983). *The Complete Book of Horse Care*. Sydney: Weldon Publishing.

Iwanowski, George. (1987). *You and Your Horse*. Pietermaritzburg: Shuter & Shooter.

Janson, Mike and Kemball-Williams, Juliana. (1996). *The Complete Book of Horse & Pony Care*. Avonmouth, Great Britain: Parragon.

Kidd, Jane. (1981). *An Illustrated Guide to Horse and Pony Care*. London: Salamander Books.

Knox-Thompson, Elaine and Dickens, Suzanne. (1998). *Pony Club Manual No. 1 & No. 2*. Auckland: Ray Richards Publishers.

McBane, Susan. (1992). *Ponywise*. Addington, Great Britain: Kenilworth Press.

McBane, Susan (ed). (1988). *The Horse and the Bit*. Ramsbury: The Crowood Press.

Pilliner, Sarah (1994). *Prepare to Win: Care of the Competition Horse*. London: B.T. Batsford.

Powell, David G. and Jackson, Stephen G. (1992). Harlow, England: Longman Scientific & Technical.

Swift, Penny and Szymanowski, Janek. (2001). *The Sporting Horse in Southern Africa*. Cape Town: BoE Private Bank.

Web Sites

www.all-about-horses.com (links to numerous sites about horse care, riding, etc)

www.aro.co.za (global racing results and racing industry information; more than 500 000 Thoroughbred pedigrees)

www.equineinfo.com (magazine-type site with lots of links)

www.horsecity.com (varied site that includes news, health information, tips and games)

www.horsedaily.com (international news for people with a passion for horses)

www.horsefun.com (links to several international `Pony Clubs; games, pictures and stories for children)

www.horsejunction@icon.co.za (comprehensive site with loads of relevant information)

www.montyroberts.com (home site of the world's most famous 'horse whisperer')

www.sportinghorse.co.za (focus on sporting horse activities; also stallion register, articles, photographic library)

www.thehorse.com (guide to equine health care)

www.worldofhorses.co.uk (news and information to keep your horse healthy)

Glossary

Horse:	Term used to describe the species, in particular, a stallion.
Foal:	Young horse under one year. May be either sex.
Colt:	Young male horse under three years.
Filly:	Young female horse under three years.
Gelding:	A castrated male horse of any age.
Mare:	Female horse of any age.
Stallion:	Uncastrated male horse.

Alfalfa: green fodder also known as lucerne

Bell boots: bell-shaped boots (or over-reach boots) to protect horses' hooves

Blanket: spotted pattern found on some Appaloosa horses

Bombproof: term used to describe a 'safe' horse or pony that can be easily be controlled by a novice rider

Bot: parasite that infests horses

Breastplate: strap designed to prevent saddles from slipping backwards

Breed: a specific equine group which has been bred selectively to achieve consistent characteristics

Bridle: headgear incorporating bit and reins, used to control horses

Brushing boots: boots used to protect the base of the leg; also called splint boots

Buck: movement of horse kicking out backwards with back arched and feet together

Cannon bone: bone between hock and fetlock

Cantle: back point of saddle

Cavesson: standard type of noseband

Clench: part of horseshoe nail that is bent over to secure the shoe

Conformation: the way a horse is formed, with particular regard to its proportions

Coolers: sweat rugs and sheets used after exercise or under thicker blankets to prevent chills

Coronet: area above the hoof at base of pastern

Crest: top line of the neck

Crupper: strap attached to the back of the saddle (cantle) and fitted under the tail to prevent the saddle from slipping forward

Croup: hindquarters or rump

Curb: chain used with curb bit that fits under the chin

Currycomb: used to rub down horse's coat; metal version used only to clean body brushes

Dandy brush: hard brush with long, stiff brushes, used to brush the coat but not the tail or mane

Dock: thick fleshy part at top of the tail

Double bridle: bridle with two bits (curb and bridoon) and two sets of reins

Drag hunting: hunting with the hounds on horseback with a scented bag instead of live quarry

Draught horse: used for pulling carts and carriages

Dressage: training in obedience and balance; developed into an elegant equestrian art and sport

Eel stripe: continuous dorsal stripe of black, brown or dun hair from neck to tail; most common in dun-coloured horses

Endurance: marathon event on horseback

Ergot: horny growth on back of fetlock joint

Eventing: competitive discipline to test horsemanship; combines dressage, show jumping and cross country

Feathers: tufts of hair on lower legs and fetlock; more pronounced in heavy horse breeds

Fetlock: ankle or joint behind pastern-joint; often with feathers

Flash: strap attached to front of caves-son noseband and fastened under chin

Flehman: action horses make by curling their lips and lifting their heads when they smell the air

Float: action of equine dentist or vet when rasping the teeth

Fly sheets: summer or day sheets used to protect horses that could develop bleaching or pigmentations in the sun

Flybucking: horse kicks out backwards while bucking

Foot feathers: *see* feathers

Forelock: mane hair that hangs over the forehead, between the ears

Frog: rubbery pad of horn in the sole of the foot that acts as a shock absorber

Fulmer: bit with cheek bars on either side; useful for horses with a tendency to nap or run out at jumps

Gag: type of bit; more severe because of its poll action

Gamgee: cotton or cotton wool encased in gauze

Gait: movement of a horse; walk, trot, canter, gallop

Girth: circumference of horse's body around its middle; also the strap that extends around the horse's stomach (or girth) to keep the saddle on

Grakle: type of noseband, with straps crossing over the front of the nose; favoured by cross-country riders

Hack: ordinary pleasure riding; also specific type of light riding horse

Halter: head collar used with a lead-rein or rope to lead or tie up a horse

Hand: term of measurement to describe horses' height; one hand (hh) equals 10.16cm (4 in)

Harness: equipment for driving horses

Hay net: net designed to hold hay, straw, lucerne, etc, so that it may be tied up off the ground

Hocks: joints between knee and fetlock

Hogged mane: mane from which all hair has been removed by clipping; also known as a roached mane in America

Hot: term describing horses/ponies that become unduly excited when ridden

Kineton noseband: design that prevents free movement of the horse's jaw; used to school horses and ponies that pull

Leopard: blanket with egg-shaped spots on white Appaloosa horses

Lucerne: plant used for fodder; known as alfalfa in some parts of the world

Lunge: circular exercise/training of horses

Marble: mottled pattern found on some Appaloosa horses

Martingale: straps used to gain extra control of the horse and stop him from raising and throwing his head; various types including standing and running

Muck out: remove droppings and clean out stables

Muzzle: area around nostrils and mouth

New Zealand rug: definitive style of waterproof cover, originally made in New Zealand; designed to enable clipped horses to stand out all year

Numnah: saddle pad or saddlecloth used under the saddle

Oat hay: juicy top stalks of oat plants

Pastern: part of foot between fetlock and hoof

Pelham: type of bit that combines a curb and bridoon or snaffle on one mouthpiece

Piebald: term (especially in the United Kingdom) to describe colouring of a pony with black and white patches on its body

Points: muzzle, mane, tail, leg extremities and tips of ears

Poll: top of horse's head

Pommel: projecting front part of saddle

Quartering: quick, basic grooming of the horse to tidy it up – particularly before exercise

Quarters: hindquarters or rump

Reining: Western riding discipline; designed to show athletic ability of a ranch-type horse in the confines of an arena similar to that used for dressage

Saddle pad: *see* numnah

Saddle tree: essential skeleton of the saddle; may be rigid or sprung

Show jumping: competitive jumping on horseback

Skewbald: term (especially in Britain) to describe colouring of a pony with coloured and white (not black) patches on its body

Snaffle: mildest bit type; snaffle bridle incorporates a snaffle bit

Snowflake: pattern of white spots concentrated on the hips of some Appaloosa horses

Stifle: joint between hip and hock

Stirrup: foot rest for rider; attached to stirrup leather attached to saddle

Stock horse: used for rounding-up sheep or cattle

Stud: breeding establishment; also refers to metal elements manufactured for use in horseshoes to help prevent slipping

Surcingle: Girth-like strap/overgirth that fits over the saddle and girth; used during eventing; blanket surcingle is used to secure rugs

Tack: abbreviation of 'tackle'; all saddlery including bridle and saddle

Tendon boots: open-fronted boots similar to brushing boots, but designed to protect tendons and fetlocks

Thrush: a bacterial infection affecting the cleft of the frog of the foot

Traces: side-straps or ropes by which horses and ponies draw carts and carriages

Turnout: general appearance of horse and rider in relation to dress, cleanliness of tack and thorough grooming

Wall: visible part of the hoof

Wall-eye: white or blue-white eye due to a lack of pigment; also called 'glass eye'

Weaving: stable vice usually caused by boredom; the horse stands at the stable door swaying from side to side

Wind sucking: a potentially harmful stable vice where the horse sucks in air

Withers: ridge between the shoulder-blades

Index